BASIC
ACCOUNTING PRINCIPLES
FOR LAWYERS

ANDERSON'S

Law School Publications

ADMINISTRATIVE LAW ANTHOLOGY
by Thomas O. Sargentich

ADMINISTRATIVE LAW: CASES AND MATERIALS
by Daniel J. Gifford

ALTERNATIVE DISPUTE RESOLUTION: STRATEGIES FOR LAW AND BUSINESS
by E. Wendy Trachte-Huber and Stephen K. Huber

AN ADMIRALTY LAW ANTHOLOGY
by Robert M. Jarvis

ANALYTIC JURISPRUDENCE ANTHOLOGY
by Anthony D'Amato

AN ANTITRUST ANTHOLOGY
by Andrew I. Gavil

APPELLATE ADVOCACY: PRINCIPLES AND PRACTICE (Second Edition)
Cases and Materials
by Ursula Bentele and Eve Cary

BASIC ACCOUNTING PRINCIPLES FOR LAWYERS:
With Present Value and Expected Value
by C. Steven Bradford and Gary A. Ames

A CAPITAL PUNISHMENT ANTHOLOGY (and Electronic Caselaw Appendix)
by Victor L. Streib

CASES AND PROBLEMS IN CRIMINAL LAW (Third Edition)
by Myron Moskovitz

THE CITATION WORKBOOK
by Maria L. Ciampi, Rivka Widerman, and Vicki Lutz

CIVIL PROCEDURE: CASES, MATERIALS, AND QUESTIONS
by Richard D. Freer and Wendy C. Perdue

COMMERCIAL TRANSACTIONS: PROBLEMS AND MATERIALS
Vol. 1: Secured Transactions Under the UCC
Vol. 2: Sales Under the UCC and the CISG
Vol. 3: Negotiable Instruments Under the UCC and the CIBN
by Louis F. Del Duca, Egon Guttman, and Alphonse M. Squillante

COMMUNICATIONS LAW: MEDIA, ENTERTAINMENT, AND REGULATION
by Donald E. Lively, Allen S. Hammond, Blake D. Morant, and Russell L. Weaver

A CONSTITUTIONAL LAW ANTHOLOGY
by Michael J. Glennon

CONSTITUTIONAL LAW: CASES, HISTORY, AND DIALOGUES
by Donald E. Lively, Phoebe A. Haddon, Dorothy E. Roberts, and Russell L. Weaver

THE CONSTITUTIONAL LAW OF THE EUROPEAN UNION
by James D. Dinnage and John F. Murphy

THE CONSTITUTIONAL LAW OF THE EUROPEAN UNION,
DOCUMENTARY SUPPLEMENT
by James D. Dinnage and John F. Murphy

CONSTITUTIONAL TORTS
by Sheldon H. Nahmod, Michael L. Wells, and Thomas A. Eaton

CONTRACTS
Contemporary Cases, Comments, and Problems
by Michael L. Closen, Richard M. Perlmutter, and Jeffrey D. Wittenberg

A CONTRACTS ANTHOLOGY (Second Edition)
by Peter Linzer

CORPORATE AND WHITE COLLAR CRIME: AN ANTHOLOGY
by Leonard Orland

A CRIMINAL LAW ANTHOLOGY
by Arnold H. Loewy

CRIMINAL LAW: CASES AND MATERIALS
by Arnold H. Loewy

A CRIMINAL PROCEDURE ANTHOLOGY
by Silas J. Wasserstrom and Christie L. Snyder

CRIMINAL PROCEDURE: ARREST AND INVESTIGATION
by Arnold H. Loewy and Arthur B. LaFrance

CRIMINAL PROCEDURE: TRIAL AND SENTENCING
by Arthur B. LaFrance and Arnold H. Loewy

ECONOMIC REGULATION: CASES AND MATERIALS
by Richard J. Pierce, Jr.

ELEMENTS OF LAW
by Eva H. Hanks, Michael E. Herz, and Steven S. Nemerson

ENDING IT: DISPUTE RESOLUTION IN AMERICA
Descriptions, Examples, Cases and Questions
by Susan M. Leeson and Bryan M. Johnston

ENVIRONMENTAL LAW (Second Edition)
Vol. 1: Environmental Decisionmaking: NEPA and the Endangered Species Act
Vol. 2: Water Pollution
Vol. 3: Air Pollution
Vol. 4: Hazardous Waste
by Jackson B. Battle, Robert L. Fischman, Maxine I. Lipeles, and Mark S. Squillace

AN ENVIRONMENTAL LAW ANTHOLOGY
by Robert L. Fischman, Maxine I. Lipeles, and Mark S. Squillace

ENVIRONMENTAL PROTECTION AND JUSTICE
Readings and Commentary on Environmental Law and Practice
by Kenneth A. Manaster

AN EVIDENCE ANTHOLOGY
by Edward J. Imwinkelried and Glen Weissenberger

FEDERAL EVIDENCE COURTROOM MANUAL
by Glen Weissenberger

FEDERAL RULES OF EVIDENCE (1996-97 Edition)
Rules, Legislative History, Commentary and Authority
by Glen Weissenberger

FEDERAL RULES OF EVIDENCE HANDBOOK (1996-97 Edition)
by Publisher's Staff

FIRST AMENDMENT ANTHOLOGY
by Donald E. Lively, Dorothy E. Roberts, and Russell L. Weaver

INTERNATIONAL ENVIRONMENTAL LAW ANTHOLOGY
by Anthony D'Amato and Kirsten Engel

INTERNATIONAL HUMAN RIGHTS: LAW, POLICY AND PROCESS (Second Edition)
by Frank C. Newman and David Weissbrodt

SELECTED INTERNATIONAL HUMAN RIGHTS INSTRUMENTS AND
BIBLIOGRAPHY FOR RESEARCH ON INTERNATIONAL HUMAN RIGHTS LAW (Second Edition)
by Frank C. Newman and David Weissbrodt

INTERNATIONAL INTELLECTUAL PROPERTY ANTHOLOGY
by Anthony D'Amato and Doris Estelle Long

INTERNATIONAL LAW ANTHOLOGY
by Anthony D'Amato

INTERNATIONAL LAW COURSEBOOK
by Anthony D'Amato

INTRODUCTION TO THE STUDY OF LAW: CASES AND MATERIALS
by John Makdisi

Continue

JUDICIAL EXTERNSHIPS: THE CLINIC INSIDE THE COURTHOUSE
by Rebecca A. Cochran

JUSTICE AND THE LEGAL SYSTEM
A Coursebook
by Anthony D'Amato and Arthur J. Jacobson

THE LAW OF DISABILITY DISCRIMINATION
by Ruth Colker

ADA HANDBOOK
Statutes, Regulations and Related Materials
by Publisher's Staff

THE LAW OF MODERN PAYMENT SYSTEMS AND NOTES
by Fred H. Miller and Alvin C. Harrell

LAWYERS AND FUNDAMENTAL MORAL RESPONSIBILITY
by Daniel R. Coquillette

MICROECONOMIC PREDICATES TO LAW AND ECONOMICS
by Mark Seidenfeld

PATIENTS, PSYCHIATRISTS AND LAWYERS
Law and the Mental Health System
by Raymond L. Spring, Roy B. Lacoursiere, M.D., and Glen Weissenberger

PROBLEMS AND SIMULATIONS IN EVIDENCE (Second Edition)
by Thomas F. Guernsey

A PRODUCTS LIABILITY ANTHOLOGY
by Anita Bernstein

PROFESSIONAL RESPONSIBILITY ANTHOLOGY
by Thomas B. Metzloff

A PROPERTY ANTHOLOGY
by Richard H. Chused

THE REGULATION OF BANKING
Cases and Materials on Depository Institutions and Their Regulators
by Michael P. Malloy

A SECTION 1983 CIVIL RIGHTS ANTHOLOGY
by Sheldon H. Nahmod

SPORTS LAW: CASES AND MATERIALS (Second Edition)
by Raymond L. Yasser, James R. McCurdy, and C. Peter Goplerud

A TORTS ANTHOLOGY
by Lawrence C. Levine, Julie A. Davies, and Edward J. Kionka

TRIAL PRACTICE
by Lawrence A. Dubin and Thomas F. Guernsey

TRIAL PRACTICE AND CASE FILES
by Edward R. Stein and Lawrence A. Dubin

TRIAL PRACTICE AND CASE FILES with *Video* Presentation
by Edward R. Stein and Lawrence A. Dubin

FORTHCOMING PUBLICATIONS

A CONFLICT OF LAWS ANTHOLOGY
by Gene R. Shreve

A CORPORATE LAW ANTHOLOGY
Franklin A. Gevurtz

CONSTITUTIONAL CONFLICTS
by Derrick A. Bell, Jr.

A FEDERAL INCOME TAX ANTHOLOGY
by Paul L. Caron, Karen C. Burke, and Grayson M.P. McCouch

Continued

PATIENTS, PSYCHIATRISTS AND LAWYERS
Law and the Mental Health System (Second Edition)
by Raymond L. Spring, Roy B. Lacoursiere, M.D., and Glen Weissenberger

PRINCIPLES OF EVIDENCE (Third Edition)
by Irving Younger, Michael Goldsmith, and David A. Sonenshein

PUBLIC CHOICE & PUBLIC LAW: READINGS AND COMMENTARY
by Maxwell L. Stearns

SCIENCE IN EVIDENCE
by David H. Kaye

UNINCORPORATED BUSINESS ENTITIES
by Larry E. Ribstein

BASIC
ACCOUNTING PRINCIPLES
FOR LAWYERS

WITH PRESENT VALUE
AND EXPECTED VALUE

C. STEVEN BRADFORD
Professor of Law
University of Nebraska

GARY ADNA AMES
Certified Public Accountant
Assistant Professor of Accounting
Illinois State University

ANDERSON PUBLISHING CO.
CINCINNATI

BASIC ACCOUNTING PRINCIPLES FOR LAWYERS

Anderson Publishing Co.
2035 Reading Road / Cincinnati, Ohio 45202
800-582-7295 / e-mail andpubco@aol.com / Fax 513-562-5430

ISBN: 0-87084-104-1

TABLE OF CONTENTS

PREFACE

It isn't easy to write about accounting. Most people prefer disease, pestilence, and even law school to reading about accounting. Many accounting books go out of their way to encourage this attitude; they are boring, pedantic,[1] and humorless. The main lesson they teach about accounting is that it's something to be avoided at all cost.

We've tried to make this book interesting and understandable for law students who have no desire to become accountants. One of us (Professor Bradford) has little formal training in accounting. He remembers what it was like to encounter this subject for the first time. The other (Professor Ames) teaches introductory accounting to undergraduates. He's constantly reminded of what it's like for students to encounter this subject for the first time.

We've tried to transform accounting concepts into clear, conversational English and to inject some humor into the subject. Accounting is dry enough; we see no reason to make it drier. And we've limited the scope of the book to the basic details that every lawyer and law student should know. This is not a treatise on accounting but a relatively short introduction to the essentials.

Our book is designed to be used for a short mini-course on accounting, or as a supplement in courses that touch on accounting issues. It is not intended to be used as the primary text for the typical two or three-credit law and accounting course, although it could be used as a supplement in such a course.

Professor Bradford thanks his colleagues at the University of Nebraska College of Law for their contributions to this book. In their defense, they try to stop his silliness, but consistently fail. Professor Bradford also thanks his wife Meg and his four wonderful children—Jason, Allison, John, and Anne. They realize Daddy is a little goofy, but they put up with him anyway. They in turn inspire Daddy to accomplish what little he accomplishes. Meg deserves a special thanks for her valuable comments on the manuscript.

Professor Ames thanks Professor Bradford, who first had the idea to write this book (and who, therefore, deserves most of the blame). He also thanks his wife Lynn and his seven (that's right, SEVEN) children: Daniel, Jessica, Tyler, Jacob, Stephen, Carly, and Rachel. Without them,

---

[1] We promise this is the last word we'll use that we had to look up to verify its meaning.

his life would be as dull and drab as every other accountant's. Because of them, he has great happiness and a longer dedication than he otherwise would have had.

Both of us are grateful to Meg Bradford, Thomas R. Craig, Bill Lyons, and Steve Willborn for reading the manuscript of this book. Their comments have made the book better. We thank the people at Anderson Publishing for helping to make this book a reality. When we first contacted them, the book was nothing more than a vague idea in our minds; Anderson helped to turn that idea into a reality. Given the state of our minds, that's quite an accomplishment. We also appreciate their patience in waiting for us to finish.

Finally, this has been a cooperative effort. Each author would like to stress that any faults in this book are solely the responsibility of the other.

Steve Bradford
Gary Adna Ames

A NOTE ABOUT FOOTNOTES

This book contains footnotes, but don't feel obligated to read them. Our footnotes aren't like the footnotes in casebooks and law reviews. You can skip our footnotes and not miss anything important. On second thought, maybe our footnotes *are* like the footnotes in casebooks and law reviews.

Our footnotes are of three types: (1) humorous comments; (2) citations; and (3) anal-retentive stuff.

1. Humorous Comments. These are the most important footnotes. In this book, we make fun of accounting, accountants, law students, professors, and everyone else we could think of to offend. Where those attempts at humor would have broken up the text, we've relegated them to the footnotes. Read these footnotes to remain sane as you learn accounting.

2. Citations. Unlike the authors of law review articles, we haven't provided a citation for everything we say including the meaning of the word "the." Citations are provided only when we're directly quoting or otherwise owe a special debt to a particular source. We have not cited all the primary accounting sources that contain the rules we're discussing; if you wanted that much detail, you wouldn't be reading this book. You can ignore our citation footnotes unless you're a law review editor and want to check their form.

3. Anal-Retentive Stuff. Occasionally, our footnotes contain qualifications or explanatory material that we thought some anal-retentive people might demand. These footnotes really aren't essential to understanding the basic principles in the text, but they make the book appear more intellectual so your law professor will require you to buy it. We sometimes begin these footnotes by telling you not to read them. If you're anal-retentive, feel free to read them. If not, ignore them.

SECTION ONE:

INTRODUCTION
TO ACCOUNTING

1

INTRODUCTION

Don't Be Scared; It's Only Accounting

Most people think that accounting (and accountants) are boring.[1] They picture grim, pale, lifeless drones in green eyeshades drearily hunched over ledger books, oblivious to the joys of life surrounding them. Several years ago, *The Wall Street Journal* published an article explaining "Why You Never Saw Charles Bronson Cast as Hero Accountant."[2] In the story, the *Journal* described how dull and boring accountants are. If you've read the *Wall Street Journal* and know how dull and boring it is, you can understand what a slap in the face this is to the accounting profession.

Because of accounting's dull reputation, lawyers and law students are reluctant to study it. They approach accounting like they approach cleaning up after the dog: they'd rather not do it and, if they have to, they know it will stink. Few lawyers or law students *want* to learn accounting. You're probably reading this book because it was assigned or because someone forced you to learn something about accounting.

But a basic knowledge of accounting is important to lawyers. Accounting issues arise in fields as diverse as corporations, criminal law, wills and trusts, family law, employment and labor law, tax law, law and economics, antitrust, commercial law, estate planning, and international law. It is difficult to avoid accounting issues in a legal career, so you need to be prepared.

Fortunately, an introduction to accounting principles doesn't have to be difficult or boring. This book is designed for law students (and lawyers) who have no background in accounting or who have forgotten what little they learned. We're not going to make you accountants.[3] When you finish this book, you won't be ready to prepare a tax return for Microsoft or General Motors. We're not even going to make you ac-

---

[1] One of the authors of this book, who has a Ph.D. in accounting, disagrees with this statement. But the other author is an attorney, and the attorney threatened to sue the accountant for all he's worth (not much) if this sentence was deleted.

[2] Lee Berton, "Why You Never Saw Charles Bronson Cast as Hero Accountant," WALL ST. J., April 26, 1984.

[3] Which should relieve you immensely. After all, who wants to be boring?

counting students.[4] This book contains less detail than you'd find in a typical undergraduate accounting book. Our goal is to teach you just enough accounting so you can understand the accounting issues that typically arise in law school.

Learning accounting is a lot like learning a foreign language.[5] Accounting, like the law, has its own jargon—the accounting equivalents of *res judicata* or *assumpsit*. To understand basic accounting, you need to learn some of the terminology and be able to speak the language. You can't read an Italian restaurant's menu without knowing Italian, and you can't read accounting statements without knowing some accounting terminology. We'll try to teach you the accounting language without forcing you to become a native.

The Purpose of Accounting

If accounting is totally new to you, you may have no idea what accounting is all about. The basic purposes of accounting are to collect, report, and analyze financial information about individuals and companies. In the remainder of this book, we will discuss the kinds of financial information accountants deal with. To put it simply, accountants are interested in what a person owns, what a person owes, and how much a person is earning. Accountants aren't interested in other information about you, like how much you weigh or the color of your eyes.[6]

The uses of accounting information are myriad. The government wants to know a person's income so it can assess an income tax. An investor wants to know a company's financial position to decide whether or not to invest in the company. A court wants to know a couple's assets and liabilities to allocate their property in a divorce. A manager of a business wants to know how profitable a product is to decide whether to keep making it. The world is filled with accounting problems, which is, of course, why you bought this book.

The Uncertainty of Accounting

Many law students, who understand clearly the uncertainty of the law, see the numbers in accounting statements and assume that accounting is nothing more than counting and mathematical calculation. Accountants are, it is commonly thought, only bean-counters.[7] We hope to destroy that myth, and show you how ambiguous and uncertain

---

[4] Accounting students are just as dull as real accountants, but less knowledgeable.

[5] In other words, just like your first year of law school.

[6] Unless, like the wife of one of the authors, you make the mistake of dating an accountant.

[7] The accountant author of the book is getting more and more irritated with the lawyer author as this chapter progresses.

accounting can be. Numbers or not, accounting is subject to uncertainty and manipulation just like the law.

Accountants like to tell a joke about three applicants being interviewed for the same job opening. The first applicant is an engineer. Her interview is going well until the interviewer's final question: "What is two plus two?" The engineer is caught a bit off-guard, but gives a rather lengthy answer using theoretical mathematics to explain why two plus two in base ten must equal four. The second person being interviewed is an attorney. Asked the same question, the attorney objects that the question is not relevant to the job in question and violates applicable federal law. The final applicant is an accountant. When the interviewer asks him, "What is two plus two?," the accountant stands up, locks the door, glances around the room, and then quietly asks the interviewer, "What do you want it to be?"

The joke is old and not terribly funny,[8] but its point is important: accounting numbers may be organized, quite legitimately, in a variety of ways. Accounting involves creativity, and that creativity makes accounting potentially dangerous. That creativity also makes it important that lawyers understand accounting.

Real-life examples of the uncertainty in accounting appear all the time, but they are seldom presented as accounting problems. For example, Winston Groom, the author of the book on which the movie *Forrest Gump* was based, sold the rights to the story to Paramount for an upfront payment plus a percentage of the movie's profits. By the middle of 1995, the movie had earned gross revenues of over $600 million, but Paramount contended that there had been no profit.[9] In the fall of 1994, the major league baseball players went on strike. The owners argued, with seeming sincerity, that the teams were not very profitable and, in some cases, teams were even losing money. The players, pointing to the success of the game, countered that the owners were engaged in some sort of financial sleight of hand.

The answer is not necessarily that anyone is being dishonest (although that's always a possibility), but that accounting numbers, like legal arguments, can be used to prove many points. (What do you want it to be?) When you finish this book, you'll understand accounting principles and terminology but, more importantly, you'll understand some of the ambiguities in accounting. You, too, may be able to ask, "What do you want it to be?"

---

[8] What do you expect from accountants?

[9] *See* John Lippman, "Author of 'Gump', Paramount in Talks Over 'Net Profit'," WALL ST. J., May 25, 1995.

2

THE BALANCE SHEET:
ASSETS, LIABILITIES, AND EQUITY

How much are you worth? Your mother, of course, thinks you're priceless,[1] but what's your financial worth? How much are you worth in dollars and cents?

For those of you whose last name is not Trump or Kennedy, the question is not too difficult and can usually be answered in a few minutes. First, make a list of everything you own that has any value— anything that can be legally sold to an unrelated third party for cash. Estimate the market value of each of those items.[2] Second, make a list of everything you owe that you will ultimately have to pay in cash. The difference between the two figures is your **net worth** or **equity**.

Let's consider an example. Jane Swift is a second-year law student at Horace's Auto Body and Law College.[3] She has a total of $300 in cash and in her checking account. She owns a car that she could sell for $2,500. She also owns a stereo, a television, and a VCR that might collectively sell for $400 at a garage sale. Her clothes, dishes, law books, and other miscellaneous items are worth about $1,400. She also has some stock that her grandparents gave her; she could sell it for $1,000. Jane has no other property or investments.[4] Accountants call all of these things of value **assets**. The total market value of Jane's assets is $5,600.

Now, let's review what Jane owes to others. She has a credit card with an outstanding balance of $475. To buy her car, she had to get a loan; she still owes $1,000 on that. Her phone bill, for $75, just arrived in the mail. Jane is one of the fortunate few who had to borrow only a

---

[1] Unless, of course, you're an accountant.

[2] "Market value" means the price you could get selling the item to someone who is not related to you and is trying to make the best deal possible. For example, how much could the item be sold for at your next garage sale?

[3] Horace's motto: We'll fix it and make somebody else pay.

[4] Jane has a boyfriend, but he doesn't count as an asset because she doesn't own him and he couldn't be sold to anyone. In any event, Jane thinks he's worthless.

small amount of money to attend law school. Her outstanding student loans currently total $2,500. Accountants call these debts **liabilities**. Jane's liabilities total $4,050.

The difference between Jane's assets and liabilities ($1,550) is her **net worth** or **equity**. Unlike many law students, Jane has a positive net worth. Her assets are worth more than her liabilities.

Accountants usually organize assets, liabilities, and net worth into a statement known as a **balance sheet**. A balance sheet for Jane would look like this:

Jane Swift
Balance Sheet
As Of February 29, 1997

Assets		Liabilities	
Cash	$300	Credit Card Debt	$475
Stock	1,000	Car Loan	1,000
Car	2,500	Phone Bill Payable	75
Electronics	400	Student Loans	2,500
Misc. Assets	1,400	Total Liabilities	$4,050
		Net Worth	
		Jane, Personal Worth	$1,550
		Total Liabilities and	
Total Assets	$5,600	Net Worth	$5,600

The balance sheet is the accounting statement that you'll probably see most often in law school. It is a static picture of the financial position of an individual or business at a particular point in time. Think of it as a financial photograph. A photograph of you taken at 7:00 a.m. would look different from a photo of you taken at 7:00 p.m.[5] Similarly, a balance sheet of a company or individual as of December 1 will look different from the same person's balance sheet at the end of December. For instance, Jane currently has a liability for her phone bill (known as a payable). When she pays the bill, she will have $75 less cash and she will no longer have a liability for it. Both her assets and her liabilities will decrease by $75. After that payment, her balance sheet will look different.

Jane's balance sheet, like all balance sheets, consists of three different sections—**assets**, **liabilities**, and **equity** or **net worth**. **Assets** are the economic resources owned by the business or individual. These can

---

[5] We'll leave it to you to decide which would look better.

be physical assets—such as buildings, merchandise, equipment, and real estate—or they can be intangible assets. Intangible assets are things of value such as patent rights, copyrights, and trademarks which have no real physical existence (although they might be represented by documents).

Assets are usually valued on the balance sheet on the basis of **historical cost**—the price the business or individual paid to acquire them (sometimes with an allowance for depreciation, which we discuss in a later chapter). The historical cost appearing on the balance sheet may have little relation to the current market value of the asset. An asset may have become obsolete since it was purchased, reducing its market value below what the company paid for it. Or, because of inflation or other changes in the market, an asset might currently be worth more than what the company paid for it. For example, if a company bought a lot in downtown Los Angeles in 1910 for $5,000, the balance sheet would list it at $5,000, even though it may now be worth many millions of dollars. The balance sheet we prepared for Jane is somewhat atypical because it lists what her property would currently sell for, not what she paid for it. Her balance sheet is not based on historical cost.

Liabilities are simply debts owed (or in some cases, expected to be owed) by the business or individual—in Jane's case, the debts she will have to repay at some time in the future.

Equity is the net worth—the difference between the assets and the liabilities:

EQUITY (OR NET WORTH) = ASSETS – LIABILITIES.

On a balance sheet, assets are usually shown on the left-hand side and liabilities and equity on the right-hand side. It's called a balance sheet because the total on the left-hand side always exactly equals the total on the right-hand side. The two sides must always balance if the balance sheet has been prepared properly. If you use a little algebra to reorganize the equation above,[6] it becomes the basic accounting equation:

ASSETS = LIABILITIES + EQUITY

Thus, by definition, the two sides of the balance sheet should always balance. If they don't, something is seriously wrong with the balance sheet (and some accountant is about to be fired).

Businesses, to determine *their* financial health, organize their financial picture in essentially the same fashion as Jane's. If a business

---

[6] Sorry. We promise not to use any more algebra in this book.

named JS Company had the same assets and liabilities that Jane has, that business would develop a balance sheet such as that shown below:

JS Company
Balance Sheet
As Of February 29, 1997

Assets		Liabilities	
Cash	$300	Short Term Loan Payable	$475
Marketable Securities	1,000	Auto Loan Payable	1,000
Automobile	2,500	Utilities Payable	75
Equipment	400	Student Loans	2,500
Misc. Assets	1,400	Total Liabilities	$4,050
		Equity	
		Net Worth	$1,550
		Total Liabilities and	
Total Assets	$5,600	Equity	$5,600

Jane's balance sheet and the JS Company balance sheet are alike except that some of the account titles are slightly different. If you can develop a balance sheet like Jane's for yourself, and understand what it means, you can understand a corporation's balance sheet. Some of the terms may be different and some of the financial instruments may be complex, but the basic principles are the same.

3

THE INCOME STATEMENT: REVENUES, EXPENSES, AND NET INCOME (LOSS)

In the last chapter, we developed a balance sheet for Jane Swift. A balance sheet, you will recall, is a financial snapshot—a picture of a person's financial position at one point in time. The balance sheet tells us very little about how the person reached that position. Jane might have lost a million dollars the day before we prepared the balance sheet or her financial position could have been stable for the last ten years. Her phone bill might be nine months overdue or she might have received it yesterday.

It's useful to view the financial condition of a business or individual over a period of time (such as a week or a month or longer) rather than at one point in time. The primary accounting statement that does this is the **Income Statement**. If the balance sheet is like a snapshot, the income statement is more like a movie. It shows what happened to the business or individual during a specified period.

Let's prepare an income statement for Jane Swift, our hypothetical law student. Assume that, after her second year of law school, Jane takes a summer job with a law firm that pays her $2,000 per month. Her only other income that summer is a quarterly dividend of $25 from her stocks, which she receives in July. Jane rents an apartment for the summer that she shares with three others. Her share of the rent is $500 per month. Her share of the monthly utilities is an additional $175. It costs Jane $50 per month to insure her car and another $125 a month for gas, oil, and maintenance. She spends $600 a month on food and has to supply her own legal pads, at a cost of $25 per month.

Jane's salary and dividend check are known as her **revenues**. Revenues are the assets that a person or business receives from selling goods or performing services. Often, as in Jane's case, revenues are in cash, but not always. Any non-cash payment for goods or services can also be revenue. In *To Kill A Mockingbird*, a farmer paid lawyer Atticus Finch with hickory nuts and turnip greens. The value of the produce would be revenue to Mr. Finch.

The costs Jane has to pay are known as her **expenses**. Expenses are the assets that a person or business uses up in producing revenues.

The difference between Jane's revenues and expenses is her **net income** (or her **net loss**, if her expenses are greater than her revenues):

NET INCOME (OR LOSS) = REVENUES – EXPENSES

An income statement has essentially three parts: a list of revenues, a list of expenses, and a calculation of the difference between the two (the net income or net loss). Jane's income statement for the month of July would look like the following:

Jane Swift
Income Statement
For the Month Ending July 31, 1997

Revenues:		
Work	$ 2,000	
Dividend	25	
Total Revenues		$2,025
Expenses:		
Rent	$ 500	
Utilities	175	
Insurance	50	
Gas & Oil	125	
Food	600	
Legal Pads	25	
Total Expenses		1,475
Net Income Before Income Taxes		$ 550
Income Taxes		410
Net Income After Income Taxes		$ 140

Jane has total revenues of $2,025 and total expenses before taxes of $1,475. Her net income before taxes is $550. However, Jane has one other expense: she has to pay taxes of $410 per month on her salary. It is customary to treat tax expenses separately like this so that you can see what happened to Jane both before and after the government took its share. Jane's net income after taxes is $140, which should be enough money to buy her law books next semester (assuming she takes only one class).

Businesses, to measure their income, organize their income statements in essentially the same way as Jane's, although some of the account names may differ. If a business, JS Company, had the same revenues and expenses as Jane, its balance sheet would look like this:

JS, Inc.
Income Statement
For the Month Ending July 31, 1997

Revenues:		
Service Revenue	$ 2,000	
Investment Revenue	25	
Total Revenues		$2,025
Expenses:		
Rent Expense	$ 500	
Utility Expense	175	
Insurance Expense	50	
Automotive Expense	125	
Entertainment Expense	600	
Supplies Expense	25	
Total Expenses		1,475
Net Income Before Taxes		$ 550
Taxes		410
Net Income After Taxes		$ 140

Note that Jane's income statement and the JS Company income statement are essentially the same. If you can develop an income statement like Jane's for yourself, and understand what it means, you can understand a large corporation's income statement.

One issue that arises in preparing the income statement concerns the appropriate period in which to include revenue and expenses. Should Jane include an expense on the income statement for the period when she receives the bill or when she pays it? Should a business include revenue in the income statement for the period when the business completes the work or should it wait until the customer pays the bill? We discuss that issue in Chapter 7, which deals with accrual and deferral.

SECTION TWO:

MORE ABOUT
THE BALANCE SHEET

4

DOUBLE-ENTRY BOOKKEEPING: HOW TRANSACTIONS AFFECT THE BALANCE SHEET

Double-Entry Bookkeeping

Balance sheets always balance. This is a result of what accountants call **double-entry bookkeeping**. Double-entry bookkeeping is accountants' primary contribution to Western civilization, surpassed in importance only by the wheel, the internal combustion engine, and, of course, Twinkies.

Double-entry bookkeeping means that every transaction produces equal and offsetting entries to a person's accounting records. For example, if you buy a computer for $2,000 cash, two accounting changes occur. The balance in your Cash account decreases by $2,000 and a new asset account called "Computers" is created, with a value of $2,000. When a company borrows $500, Cash increases by $500 and a liability account—probably Notes Payable—increases by $500. This double-entry system guarantees that the company's accounting records will balance.

Examples

To understand the double-entry bookkeeping system and how the balance is maintained, let's consider a few simple examples of how a balance sheet might change over time. Companies ordinarily do not prepare a new balance sheet after every transaction in which they're involved. Instead, they keep accounting records that reflect all of their transactions, and use those records to prepare a balance sheet only as needed. However, to illustrate how the double-entry system works, we'll prepare a new balance sheet after each transaction.

Assume that an individual invests $60,000 of his cash to start a new business. Before the initial investment, the business did not exist. It had nothing—no assets, no liabilities, no owner's equity. The cash the owner contributed is an asset, which is reflected on the left-hand side of the balance sheet. The business has no liabilities yet, so the amount of Owner's Equity—the difference between assets and liabilities—is the full $60,000.

17

The entry to the new company's accounting journal[1] to reflect this transaction would look like this:

Cash	60,000	
Owner's Equity		60,000

This tells the accountant that $60,000 needs to be added to the company's Cash account and $60,000 needs to be added to its Owner's Equity account. Notice that the numbers in this entry are in two columns, one indented slightly to the left and the other to the far right. For asset accounts like Cash that appear on the left-hand side of the balance sheet, a left column entry like this indicates an increase and a right column entry indicates a reduction. For accounts like Owner's Equity that appear on the right-hand side of the balance sheet, a right column entry like this indicates an increase and a left column entry indicates a reduction. Accountants call left column entries **debits**. They call right column entries **credits**.[2]

A balance sheet prepared for this business after the initial investment and before anything else happened would look like this:

Assets		*Liabilities*	$0
Cash	$60,000	*Owner's Equity*	60,000
		Total Liabilities	
Total Assets	$60,000	and Owner's Equity	$60,000

Notice the double-entry handling of this transaction. The $60,000 addition to the Cash account and the $60,000 addition to the Owner's Equity account offset each other, so the balance sheet balances.

If the new company purchased land for $21,000 cash, the accounting journal entry would look like this:

Land	$21,000	
Cash		$21,000

Land is an asset account that appears on the left-hand side of the balance sheet, so an addition to it appears in the left column of the

---

[1] An accounting journal is just a chronological recording of the company's financial transactions. Think of it as the company's financial diary.

[2] Debits include increases in asset accounts, reductions of liability or equity accounts, and increases in revenue accounts. Credits include reductions in asset accounts, increases in liability or equity acounts, and increases in expense accounts.

journal entry. Cash is also an asset account on the left-hand side of the balance sheet, so a reduction of Cash appears in the right column of the journal entry.

After the purchase, the company's balance sheet would look like this:

Assets		Liabilities	$0
Cash	$39,000	Owner's Equity	60,000
Land	21,000	Total Liabilities	
Total Assets	$60,000	and Owner's Equity	$60,000

The Cash account is reduced by $21,000, the amount of cash used to purchase the land. A new Land account has been created to show the new asset; the accounting value of that asset is its cost, $21,000. The total on the left-hand side of the balance sheet has not changed; one asset (Land) has merely been substituted for another (Cash). Nothing has happened to the right-hand side of the balance sheet. The company paid cash for the land, so there still are no liabilities. Owner's Equity has not changed; the difference between assets and liabilities is still the same.

What if, instead of paying cash for the land, the company borrowed $21,000 from the bank and signed a note agreeing to repay the $21,000 in one year? After the land purchase, the balance sheet would look like this:

Assets		Liabilities	
Cash	$60,000	Note Payable	$21,000
Land	$21,000	Owner's Equity	60,000
		Total Liabilities	
Total Assets	$81,000	and Owner's Equity	$81,000

As before, a new asset has been acquired; a new account, Land, is created with a value of $21,000. The Cash account did not change because the company paid no cash. However, the company has taken on a new liability—the note—which must be paid at some time in the future. That liability is reflected on the liability side of the balance sheet by the addition of a Note Payable account in the amount of $21,000. The amount in the Owner's Equity account has not changed because the difference between assets and liabilities is still the same. Again, double-entry bookkeeping has preserved the balance.

The related entry to the company's accounting journal would look like this:

Land	$21,000	
Note Payable		$21,000

Assume that the company now sells the land to someone for $25,000 cash, producing a profit of $4,000. The balance sheet would then look like this:

Assets		Liabilities	
Cash	$85,000	Note Payable	$21,000
		Owner's Equity	$64,000
Total Assets	$85,000	Total Liabilities and Owner's Equity	$85,000

The company no longer owns the land, so the Land account disappears from the left-hand side of the balance sheet. The company has received $25,000 cash, so that amount is added to the Cash account. The result is a net increase of $4,000 on the asset side of the balance sheet. This $4,000 profit on the sale of the land increases the difference between assets and liabilities. The Equity account therefore must increase by $4,000 to reflect the profit.

The related entry in the company's accounting journal would look like this:

Cash	$25,000	
Land		$21,000
Owner's Equity		$4,000

In this case, double-entry bookkeeping actually involves not two, but three, entries. Two right column entries are required to balance the left column addition to the Cash account.

In the real world, accounting for this profitable transaction would be a little more complicated. The profit would first affect the Income Statement as a gain and, at the end of the period, net income from the

Income Statement would increase the amount in the Owner's Equity account.

Assume next that the owner of our hypothetical company needs some money, so he withdraws $10,000 cash from the business. The balance sheet would then look like this:

Assets		Liabilities	
Cash	$75,000	Note Payable	$21,000
		Owner's Equity	54,000
		Total Liabilities	
Total Assets	$75,000	and Owner's Equity	$75,000

The amount in the cash account is $10,000 less because of the withdrawal. This reduces the difference between assets and liabilities by $10,000, so the amount in the equity account must also decrease by $10,000. In essence, the owner has withdrawn some of his equity in the business. The related journal entry would look like this:

Owner's Equity	$10,000	
Cash		$10,000

Finally, assume that the company pays off the note it signed to purchase the land. The balance sheet would then look like this:

Assets		Liabilities	$ 0
Cash	$54,000	Owner's Equity	54,000
		Total Liabilities	
Total Assets	$54,000	and Owner's Equity	$54,000

The Cash account is reduced by $21,000, the amount of cash used to repay the loan. (To simplify things, we're assuming no interest was paid.) As a result of the repayment, the liability, Note Payable, has disappeared. Since Assets and Liabilities have each been reduced by the same amount ($21,000), the difference between the two is unchanged and the amount in the Equity account stays the same. The balance sheet continues to balance.

The related entry to the company's accounting journal looks like this:

Note Payable	$21,000	
Cash		$21,000

T-Accounts

Sometimes, accounting changes like those discussed in this chapter are illustrated using what are known as **T-accounts**. No company actually uses T-accounts in its record keeping, but you will see them in textbooks, primarily because they make accounting more mysterious to a lay person like you, justifying the fees accountants charge.[3]

T-accounts are a way to keep a running total of the amount in each account (such as Cash, Land, Notes Payable, and Owner's Equity). They're called T-accounts because they're shaped like a "T."[4] The T-accounts, like the balance sheet, must balance. Every entry to the left-hand side of one T-account must be matched by a corresponding entry to the right-hand side of some other T-account. And the total of the left-hand sides of all the T-accounts must equal the total of the right-hand sides of all the T-accounts.

Consider again the series of transactions we discussed earlier in this chapter. First, an individual contributes $60,000 cash to a new business. Two accounts are affected, Cash and Owner's Equity:

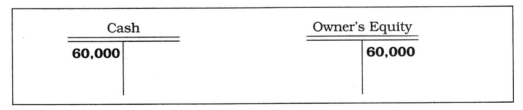

The Cash account appears on the left-hand, asset side of the balance sheet. Additions to a left-hand side account appear on the left of the T-account. Reductions in a left-hand side account appear on the right of the T-account. Thus, 60,000 on the left of the Cash T-account indicates an addition of $60,000 to Cash. Owner's Equity appears on the right-hand side of the balance sheet. Additions to a right-hand-side account appear on the right of the T-account. Reductions in a right-hand-side account appear on the left of the T-account. Thus, 60,000 on the right of the Owner's Equity T-account indicates an increase of $60,000 in Owner's Equity. Note that the total of all the left-hand sides and the

---

[3] As an aspiring lawyer, you should find this concept very familiar.
[4] And you thought accountants had no imagination.

total of all the right-hand sides are equal. T-accounts, like the balance sheet, must balance.

Next, the company borrows $21,000 from a bank, signing a one-year note, and uses the loan to buy land:

Cash	Land	Note Payable	Owner's Equity
60,000	**21,000**	**21,000**	60,000

The Land account increases by $21,000. Since Land is an asset account on the left-hand side of the balance sheet, an increase appears on the left side of the T-account. The Note Payable account also increases by $21,000. Since Note Payable is a liability account on the right-hand side of the balance sheet, an increase appears on the right side of the T-account. Again, the total of all the left sides ($81,000) equals the total of all the right sides ($81,000); the T-accounts balance.

Next, the company sells the land for $25,000:

Cash	Land	Note Payable	Owner's Equity
60,000	21,000	21,000	60,000
25,000	**21,000**		**4,000**

Cash increases by $25,000, the Land account is reduced by its full balance—$21,000, and the Owner's Equity account increases by $4,000, the amount of the profit. If you total all the left sides and all the right sides, you'll see that the T-accounts still balance.

Next, the owner withdraws $10,000 cash from the business:

Cash	Land	Note Payable	Owner's Equity
60,000	21,000	21,000	60,000
25,000	21,000		4,000
10,000			10,000

Cash is reduced by $10,000, and Owner's Equity is reduced by $10,000. Finally, the company pays the note:

Cash		Land		Note Payable		Owner's Equity	
60,000		21,000			21,000		60,000
25,000			21,000	**21,000**			4,000
	10,000					10,000	
	21,000						

Cash is reduced by $21,000 and the Note Payable account is reduced by its full amount, $21,000.

T-accounts keep a running total of what is in each account. To prepare a balance sheet, all you need to do is total the figures in each T-account. To total a T-account, you simply add the numbers on each side of each T, and calculate the difference between the two sides. The difference, which appears on the side of the T-account with the larger number, is the balance in the account. The balances in each of the T-accounts below are identical to the numbers that appear on the final balance sheet we prepared earlier in this chapter:

Cash		Land		Note Payable		Owner's Equity	
60,000		21,000			21,000		60,000
25,000			21,000	21,000			4,000
	10,000					10,000	
	21,000						
54,000		**0**		**0**			**54,000**

If you go back and total the amounts in the T-accounts after each transaction, you'll see that, at each step, the totals match the figures in the corresponding balance sheets we prepared earlier.

5

THE EQUITY SECTION OF THE BALANCE SHEET

Introduction

As we explained earlier, the equity section of the balance sheet represents the difference between the assets and liabilities of the business or individual—the net worth. The basic accounting equation is: Assets - Liabilities = Equity. If the business has more assets than liabilities, the total in the equity section is positive. If the business has more liabilities than assets, the total in the equity section is negative.

Net income increases the amount in the equity section; net losses reduce the amount in the equity section. To understand why, recall that revenues are the assets a person or business receives for goods or services and expenses are the assets used up to produce revenues. A person has net income for a period if revenues exceed expenses—when the value of the assets coming in exceeds the value of the assets going out. Equity, the difference between the person's total assets and total liabilities, increases by the amount of the net income. A person has a net loss for a period if expenses exceed revenues—when the value of the assets coming in is less than the value of the assets going out. Equity decreases by the amount of the net loss.

The appearance of the equity section of the balance sheet varies depending on the organizational form of the business. Corporations, partnerships, and sole proprietorships all present equity differently. You'll learn the differences among corporations, partnerships, and sole proprietorships in a Corporations or Business Associations course. Luckily, you don't need all the legal details to understand how they account for equity differently.

Sole Proprietorships and Individuals

The simplest accounting for equity is for an individual or a sole proprietorship. A sole proprietorship is a business with only one owner that has not taken the legal steps necessary to form some other kind of organization. The equity section of the balance sheet of an individual or a sole proprietorship is simply one line called Equity or Net Worth. The balance sheet we prepared for Jane Swift in Chapter 2 is a good example of the equity section of an individual's balance sheet.

25

Income increases a sole proprietorship's Equity account; losses reduce the Equity account. Investments of additional money or withdrawals of money by the owner of the sole proprietorship also affect the
equity account. Withdrawals or investments of capital by the owner of
a business are not revenues or expenses and do not directly affect net
income. A withdrawal of capital is not an expense because the withdrawal has nothing to do with producing income. Similarly, an investment of additional money in the business is not revenue because it
doesn't result from the productive activities of the business—selling
goods or rendering services. However, when the owner invests cash or
property in the business, the difference between assets and liabilities
increases, so the Equity account increases by the amount of the contribution. Similarly, when the owner withdraws cash or property from the
business, the Equity account decreases by the amount of the withdrawal.

Partnerships

A business with more than one owner may be a partnership. If so, the
co-owners of the business are called partners. In a partnership, a separate
equity account is maintained for each partner. Equity may appear as a
single line on the balance sheet, but, at least internally, the partnership
maintains separate equity accounts for each partner. The equity section
of a partnership balance sheet might look something like this:

Equity	
Partner Jones	$10,000
Partner Smith	5,000
Partner Brown	2,000

When a partner invests cash or property in the business, *that partner's* equity account usually increases by the amount of the investment.
When a partner withdraws cash or property from the business, *that
partner's* equity account decreases by the amount of the withdrawal.
Income is allocated to each partner's equity account according to the
percentage of profits each partner is entitled to (as determined in a
partnership agreement or by law). Losses are allocated to each partner's
account according to each partner's responsibility for losses (again, as
determined in a partnership agreement or by law). For example, if the
net income of the partnership is $10,000, and the partnership agreement
provides that Jones will receive 50 percent of the profits, Smith 25
percent, and Brown 25 percent, the equity section we showed in the
example above would change to the following:

Equity	
Partner Jones	$15,000
Partner Smith	7,500
Partner Brown	4,500

The amount in Jones' equity account increased by $5,000, 50 percent of the profits. The amounts in Smith's and Brown's equity accounts increased by $2,500 each, since each is entitled to 25 percent of the profits.

Corporations

The most complicated treatment of equity is when the business is organized as a corporation. Equity investments in a corporation are represented by shares of stock. When a person invests in a corporation, he receives shares of the corporation's stock and is known as a shareholder or stockholder. The shares of stock represent the investor's interest in the assets and profits of the corporation.

Unlike partnerships, corporations do not create a separate equity account for each investor. A corporation does, however, have more than one equity account. It is customary for corporations to segregate the equity portion of the balance sheet into at least three accounts. Accountants and everyone else in the world other than lawyers call those accounts: (1) **Capital Stock** or **Common Stock**, (2) **Additional Paid-in Capital** or **Paid-in Capital in Excess of Par Value**, and (3) **Retained Earnings**. Legal sources, in their unending quest to be unintelligible, sometimes give different names to these accounts. The following table shows the proper accounting names of these corporate equity accounts and their legal equivalents:

Corporate Equity Accounts

PROPER ACCOUNTING NAME	LEGAL NAME
Capital Stock or Common Stock	Stated Capital
Additional Paid-in Capital or Paid-in Capital in Excess of Par Value	Capital Surplus
Retained Earnings	Earned Surplus

The following sections discuss how to allocate equity among these accounts. We'll use the proper accounting names of these accounts and you can refer to the table for a translation if you need one.

Capital Stock and Additional Paid-in Capital

The amounts in both the Capital Stock and Additional Paid-in Capital accounts are based on the price the corporation receives when it sells its stock to investors. The total in the two accounts is the total amount for which the corporation sold the stock. If, for example, a corporation sells 10,000 shares of stock to the public at a price of $50 per share, it receives a total of $500,000. This $500,000 must be allocated between the Capital Stock and Additional Paid-in Capital accounts.[1]

The allocation of the proceeds from the sale of stock between those two accounts depends on whether the stock has a ***par value***. Par value is a rather arbitrary value assigned to each type of stock by the corporation that is less (usually significantly less) than the price for which the corporation sells the stock. Depending on the jurisdiction and the desires of the corporation, a corporation's stock may or may not have a par value. For our purposes, it's not necessary that you be familiar with the concept of par value. It's just important that you understand that some stock has a par value and some does not.

If the corporate stock has a par value, the amount of the par value paid by the shareholder to the corporation is added to the Capital Stock account. The excess of the purchase price over the par value is added to the Additional Paid-in Capital account, which explains this account's alternative name, Paid-in Capital in Excess of Par Value. Assume, for example, that an investor pays $100 cash for a single share of stock that has a $10 par value. The following changes would occur on the balance sheet:

Assets	Equity
Cash +$100	Capital Stock +$10
	Additional Paid-in Capital +$90

The corporation has $100 more cash as a result of the sale of stock, and this is reflected on the asset side of the balance sheet. For the balance sheet to balance, there must be an offsetting entry on the right-hand side of the balance sheet. The par value amount ($10) is added to the Capital Stock account. The remainder ($90) is added to the Additional Paid-in Capital account.

Some stock, called ***no par*** stock, has no stated par value. The corporation may still choose to allocate the purchase price between the Capital

---

[1] The balance sheet would still balance because the $500,000 cash received by the company would be added to the asset, Cash, on the left-hand side of the balance sheet.

Stock and Additional Paid-in Capital accounts, but the amount to be allocated to each account is usually left to the discretion of the corporation's board of directors. The amount allocated to the Capital Stock account is called the **stated value**. The amount of the purchase price above the stated value is allocated to the Additional Paid-in Capital account, which in these circumstances is sometimes called **Paid-in Capital in Excess of Stated Value**. If the corporation does not make such an allocation for no-par stock, the entire price is allocated to the Capital Stock account.

Retained Earnings

The third corporate capital account is **Retained Earnings**. The Retained Earnings account, unlike the other capital accounts, has nothing to do with the price at which a company sells stock to its shareholders. The figure in the Retained Earnings account results primarily from the cumulative profits and losses of the corporation. If the business has net income, its excess of assets over liabilities increases, and the amount in the Retained Earnings account must increase by the amount of the income. If the business has a net loss, its excess of assets over liabilities decreases, and the amount in the Retained Earnings account must decline by the amount of the loss. If the corporation has suffered a net loss since its inception and its total liabilities exceed its total assets, it is possible for the figure in the Retained Earnings account to be a negative number. Accountants usually indicate a negative number by bracketing the number with parentheses. Thus, ($2,000) indicates a negative $2000. When the Retained Earnings account has a negative balance, it is usually called **Accumulated Deficit**.

Let's consider an example. Assume that the balance sheet of a newly created company looks like this:

Assets		Liabilities and Shareholders' Equity	
Cash	$ 1,000	Liabilities	
Building	10,000	Notes Payable	$5,000
Equipment	2,000	Shareholder's Equity	
		Capital Stock	500
		Additional Paid-in Capital	7,500
		Retained Earnings	0
TOTAL	$13,000	TOTAL	$13,000

We can tell by looking at the Capital Stock and Additional Paid-in Capital accounts in the equity section of this balance sheet that the company sold its stock for $8,000, $500 of which is the stock's par value. We know from the Notes Payable account that the company also borrowed $5,000 and has signed notes promising to repay that money sometime in the future. Looking at the asset side of the balance sheet, we see that the company has used the $13,000 it received from the stock sales and borrowing to purchase a building for $10,000 and equipment for $2000, leaving it with $1,000 cash.

Assume that the company's first year is profitable; it has a net income of $7,500. To make it simpler, let's assume that its income was all in cash. The company uses $5,000 of that cash to pay off the notes, and keeps the remaining $2,500. Its balance sheet now looks like this:

Assets		Liabilities and Shareholders' Equity	
Cash	$ 3,500	Liabilities	$ 0
Building	10,000	Shareholder's Equity	
Equipment	2,000	Capital Stock	500
		Additional Paid-in Capital	7,500
		Retained Earnings	7,500
TOTAL	$15,500	TOTAL	$15,500

As the result of the net income, the excess of assets over liabilities increased by $7,500. The Retained Earnings account increased by $7,500 to reflect that income.

Assume that the following year is disastrous for the corporation. It has a net loss of $10,000. The $3,500 cash the corporation had on hand at the end of the first year was spent and the corporation had to borrow $6,500 from the bank just to pay its bills. Its balance sheet now looks like this:

Assets		Liabilities and Shareholders' Equity	
Cash	$ 0	Liabilities	
Building	10,000	Bank Loan Payable	6,500
Equipment	2,000	Shareholder's Equity	
		Capital Stock	500
		Additional Paid-in Capital	7,500
		Accumulated Deficit	(2,500)
TOTAL	$12,000	TOTAL	$12,000

As a result of the loss, the excess of assets over liabilities fell by $10,000. The Retained Earnings account was reduced by $10,000 to reflect that loss. Since the opening balance in the account was only $7,500, the balance is now a negative $2,500, with the negative balance indicated by the use of parentheses. Since the balance in the Retained Earnings account is negative, it is now labelled "Accumulated Deficit" rather than "Retained Earnings." The Capital Stock and Additional Paid-in Capital accounts are unchanged. All accounting profits and losses are reflected in the retained earnings account, so that the other two accounts continue to reflect the amounts paid for the corporation's stock.

Dividends paid by the corporation also affect the equity accounts. Dividends, for those unfamiliar with the term, are distributions to the shareholders, usually made from the earnings of the business. Dividends are one of the ways a corporation gets the profits of the business to the shareholders. When a cash dividend is paid, two changes occur. First, the amount in the Cash account is reduced by the amount paid. Second, the amount in the Retained Earnings account is reduced by the amount of the dividend. The key to remembering this is to focus on the word "retained" in Retained Earnings; once those earnings are distributed to the stockholders, they are no longer "retained" by the corporation.

Statement of Stockholders' Equity

Corporations' financial statements usually contain an accounting statement called the **Statement of Stockholders' Equity** or the **Statement of Capital Changes**. The Statement of Stockholders' Equity traces changes in the equity accounts over the accounting periods covered by the statement. The following is a simple example of such a statement:

	Common Stock	Addit'l Paid-In Capital	Retained Earnings
STATEMENT OF STOCKHOLDERS' EQUITY			
(All numbers are in millions)			
Balance as of Jan. 1, 1995	25	175	100
Net Income (or Loss)			40
Common Stock Dividends			(25)
Common Stock Issued	10	70	
Balance as of Dec. 31, 1995	35	245	115
Net Income (or Loss)			(10)
Common Stock Dividends			(15)
Common Stock Repurchased	(5)	(35)	
Balance as of Dec. 31, 1996	30	210	90

It is common to show more than one year's results in the Statement of Stockholders' Equity. This statement shows changes to the company's equity accounts in both 1995 and 1996. The first line of the statement indicates the balance in the company's capital accounts as of January 1, 1995—the starting point. The Capital Stock balance, which this statement lists simply as "Common Stock," was $25 million, the Additional Paid-in Capital balance was $175 million, and there was $100 million in Retained Earnings. The next three lines show changes to these accounts during 1995. The "Net Income" line indicates that, in 1995, the company's net income was $40 million; the Retained Earnings account increased by this amount. The company paid dividends to its shareholders of $25 million. This reduced the amount of Retained Earnings. The "Common Stock Issued" line shows that the company issued additional common stock for $80 million; $10 million of that amount was allocated to Capital Stock, with the remainder allocated to Additional Paid-in Capital. As a result of the changes, the balances at the end of 1995, represented by the fifth line of the statement, were $35 million in Capital Stock, $245 million in Additional Paid-in Capital, and $115 million in Retained Earnings.

The subsequent lines on the statement show changes to the equity accounts in 1996. The company had a net loss of $10 million in 1996, reducing the balance in Retained Earnings by that amount. The company paid $15 million in dividends, further reducing the amount in the Retained Earnings account. The company also repurchased some of its stock from its shareholders. The Capital Stock and Additional Paid-in Capital accounts have been reduced to reflect that this stock is no longer outstanding. The final line of the statement indicates the equity account balances as of the end of 1996: $30 million in Capital Stock, $210 million in Additional Paid-in Capital, and $90 million in Retained Earnings.

6

INSOLVENCY

Two Types of Insolvency

Insolvency is an accounting concept of which many lawyers and law students have at least a general understanding. "Insolvent" is a technical accounting term meaning you're broke. However, many people are unable to define insolvency and they often don't realize that insolvency has two very different meanings. With the benefit of this absolutely fantastic introduction to accounting principles,[1] you can be more sophisticated than most people.

One type of insolvency, **balance sheet insolvency**, focuses on the balance sheet, and compares the total dollar amount of assets to the total dollar amount of liabilities. If total liabilities on the balance sheet exceed total assets, the total of the equity accounts is negative, and the person or business is insolvent in this balance sheet, or equity, sense of insolvency. If total assets exceed total liabilities, the total of the equity accounts is positive, and the person or business is solvent in this balance sheet sense.

The second type of insolvency, **cash flow insolvency**, focuses on a person's cash flow—whether the person has sufficient cash to pay his obligations as they become due. A person who has sufficient funds to pay his debts as they become due is solvent in this cash flow sense. A person who has insufficient funds to pay his debts as they become due is insolvent in this sense.

Examples

The following two examples may make the difference between balance sheet insolvency and cash flow insolvency clearer.[2]

Consider first the balance sheet of Sam Smith:

Assets		Liabilities	
Cash	$ 100	Short-Term Debt	$30,000
Car	20,000	Equity	140,100
House	$150,000		
TOTAL	$170,100	TOTAL	$170,100

---

[1] Rush out and buy copies for your friends and relatives before they're all gone!
[2] Or they may not. We disclaim all warranties, express or implied.

Sam is solvent in the balance sheet, or equity, sense. His total assets ($170,100) are significantly greater than his total liabilities ($30,000), leaving a positive amount of $140,100 in equity.

Sam may not be solvent in the cash flow sense. Sam owes $30,000 in short-term debt (debt due in the near future) and has only $100 cash available to pay it. It's possible that Sam's cash shortage is only temporary; he might receive $30,000 cash before the debt is due. If so, he's not insolvent in the cash flow sense; he will have cash sufficient to pay the debt when it becomes due. If Sam doesn't expect to receive any cash before the debt is due, he still might be able to pay the debt by selling his house or car or by borrowing money. But it takes time to sell a house or car and the debt might be due before Sam could complete the sale. And he might not be able to find anyone willing to lend him money. If Sam can't come up with enough cash to pay the debt when it becomes due, Sam is insolvent in the cash flow sense. Notice that it is possible for Sam to be solvent in one way—the balance sheet sense—but insolvent in another way—the cash flow sense.

Consider a second example involving a person who is in exactly the opposite situation—insolvent in the balance sheet sense but not in the cash flow sense. Assume that Joe Jones has the following balance sheet:

Assets		Liabilities	
Cash	$20,000	Short-Term Debt	$10,000
Car	15,000	Long-Term Debt	50,000
		Equity	(25,000)
TOTAL	$35,000	TOTAL	$35,000

Joe is insolvent in the balance sheet sense. His total assets ($35,000) are less than his total liabilities ($60,000), resulting in a negative figure in the Equity account (-$25,000). But Joe may not be insolvent in the cash flow sense. He only owes $10,000 in the short term, and he has $20,000 cash available, more than enough to pay that debt. Joe does not presently have enough cash to pay the $50,000 long-term debt, but, since it's long-term debt, he doesn't have to pay it now. The only issue is whether he will have enough cash to pay this debt when it becomes due. If Joe expects to receive sufficient cash by the time the debt is due, he is not insolvent in the cash flow sense.

The Insolvencies of Law Students

Many law students get to experience the joys of both cash flow insolvency and balance sheet insolvency. During law school, many law students find it hard to come up with sufficient cash to pay their bills on time. They are insolvent or nearly insolvent in the cash flow sense. By the time they exit law school, many law students are insolvent in the balance sheet sense. Because of the substantial debt they incurred to go to law school, their liabilities exceed their assets (because the law degree isn't usually treated as a balance sheet asset). They have a negative net worth. But, if they are lucky enough to find a good legal job on graduation, they're probably no longer insolvent in the cash flow sense. The income they will receive from working 100 billable hours a week as associates at high-priced law firms will be more than enough to pay their law school debts as they become due.[3]

---

[3] If, on the other hand, they're working as assistant managers at McDonald's because they couldn't find a law-related job, they may still be insolvent in the cash flow sense. Their income may not be sufficient to repay their substantial student loans and they'll use what they learned in that bankruptcy course sooner than they expected.

SECTION THREE:

ACCRUAL, DEFERRAL, AND CASH FLOW

7

ACCRUAL AND DEFERRAL

Introduction to the Accrual Method of Accounting

Every expense paid in advance creates what is in essence an asset. When a company pays its May rent in February, it has created a claim to occupy the rented space in May, an asset that will be used in the future. That asset may not last for very long, but it is nevertheless an asset.

Conversely, almost every asset is in essence a prepaid expense. When a company buys a truck that will last for twenty years, it has paid in advance for the use of the truck for the next twenty years. Whether the asset is prepaid rent or a truck, the asset will eventually be consumed in a future accounting period or periods to produce income. The cost of the asset is an expense of producing the income in those future periods.

Payments for expenses and for the purchase of assets may be accounted for in two very different ways: on a *cash basis* or on an *accrual basis*. Both are ways of determining a company's net income; the difference between them is one of timing. Net income, you will recall, is measured for a particular period: the income statement presents a company's or individual's income for a specified period of time. The cash basis of accounting and the accrual basis of accounting sometimes allocate revenue and expenses to different periods, resulting in different net incomes (or losses).

The *cash basis* of accounting is the easiest to understand. It focuses on the movement of cash and allocates revenues and expenses to the accounting period in which cash revenues are received or expenses are paid. When a customer pays for goods or services, the cash payment is allocated to revenue and increases the company's net income for that period. When the company actually delivers the goods or performs the services is irrelevant. It doesn't matter if the goods were delivered in prior periods or aren't to be manufactured and delivered to the customer until sometime in the future. Similarly, when the company pays an expense, that expense is charged against income. When the company receives the benefit of the payment is irrelevant. If, for example, on January 2, 1997, a company pays $30,000 for its office rent for the next five years, the entire $30,000 is treated as an expense in 1997. The benefit of the payment will be received over the five years for which rent was paid, but the entire payment is treated as an expense for 1997 when it is paid. All that matters using the cash basis is when the cash changes hands.

The **accrual basis** does not look to when cash is received or paid. In the accrual system, revenues are recognized when they are earned by sales or services, not when payment is received. If the company delivered goods in 1996, the revenue is recognized in 1996, even if the customer didn't pay until 1997. Similarly, in the accrual system, expenses are charged against income in the period that those expenses provide benefits, not when they are paid. Thus, in the case of the pre-paid rent, one-fifth of the $30,000 payment would be treated as an expense in each of the five years for which rent was paid.

In the accrual system, revenue and expenses may be **accrued** or **deferred**. Allocating revenue or expenses to the income statement before the cash actually changes hands (before the cash is collected in the case of revenues or before the cash is paid in the case of expenses) is known as **accrual**. Allocating revenues or expenses to the income statement in a period later than the period in which cash actually changes hands (after the cash is collected in the case of revenue or after the cash is paid in the case of expenses) is known as **deferral**. Although the method itself is known as the accrual method, it includes both accrual and deferral.

Most large or mid-sized businesses use the accrual method of accounting, but many individuals and professionals (such as doctors and lawyers) use the cash method. Accountants believe the accrual method provides a more accurate financial picture of a business because it more appropriately matches expenses to the revenues they produce.

Examples of Accrual and Deferral

Some examples may help you understand accrual and deferral.

1.   Accrued Income. A client agrees to pay his lawyer's fee upon completion of a case. The lawyer successfully completes the case and sends the client a bill on November 15, 1996, but the client does not pay until February 1, 1997. The lawyer's work was done and the fee earned as of November 15, but the cash was not received until the following year. Using the cash basis of accounting, the fee would be revenue for the year 1997, when the client paid. Using the accrual basis, the fee would be accrued and treated as revenue for 1996, the year the work was completed and the fee was earned. The fee would be accrued to 1996, even though it was not collected in 1996.

2.   Accrued Expense. A lawyer orders one month's supply of legal pads on October 1, 1996. The pads are delivered to the lawyer in October and are gone by the end of the year. However, the lawyer has financial difficulties and doesn't pay the bill until January, 1997. Using the cash basis of accounting, the cost of the legal pads would be an expense in 1997, the year in which the bill was paid. Using the accrual basis, the cost of the pads would be an expense in 1996, the period during which the pads benefitted the lawyer. The expense would be accrued to 1996.

3. *Deferred Income.* On October 12, 1996, a client pays a lawyer a cash fee of $1,000 to represent the client at a hearing in March, 1997. The lawyer does no work on the case in 1996, but represents the client at the hearing in March. Using the cash basis of accounting, the fee would be revenue in the year in which the cash was paid, 1996. Using the accrual basis, the fee would not be revenue until 1997, when the lawyer did all the work and actually earned the fee. The revenue would be deferred until 1997.

4. *Deferred Expense.* After receiving a large contingent fee, a lawyer prepays the rent on his office for the next six years. Using the cash basis of accounting, the entire rent payment would be an expense in the year in which it was paid. Using the accrual basis, the rent payment would be allocated over the next six years according to the amount of rent due in each year. The expense would be deferred to the periods when the benefit of the rent payment is received.

Accounting for Accrual and Deferral Items

1. Deferred Income

When revenue is deferred, the business has received the cash, but it will not be recognized as revenue until a later accounting period. Assume that a business has received $100 cash for work it has not yet performed. Using the accrual system of accounting, the $100 has not yet been earned, so this income must be deferred to a later accounting period. But how is this accounted for? Obviously, the receipt of the cash increases the Cash account by $100. The offsetting entry cannot be to Revenue, because the revenue is not to be recognized in this accounting period. Instead, the $100 is added to an account with a name like Unearned Revenue or Deferred Revenue. This account is on the liability side of the balance sheet because the company is obligated to do something before the income is earned. Thus, the balance sheet changes as follows:

Assets		Liabilities and Equity
Cash	+$100	Unearned or Deferred Revenue +$100

When this income is earned by performance, the unearned or deferred revenue account is reduced by the $100, and $100 is added to revenue for that period.

2. *Deferred Expenses*

When an expense is deferred, the business has paid the cash, but the payment will not be recognized as an expense until some future period. Assume, for example, that in 1996 a business prepays its 1997 rent in the amount of $5,000. One of the accounting entries is obvious: the Cash account must be reduced by $5,000 because the business now has $5,000 less cash. But what is the offsetting entry so the books continue to balance? In essence, the business has a new asset that it will use at sometime in the future—the ability to occupy the rented space in 1997. A new asset account called Prepaid Rent is created, and $5,000 is added to this account.

What happens in the 1997 accounting period when the company uses this asset? The $5,000 is an expense for the 1997 period that should be deducted in calculating net income for that period. In 1997, the $5,000 is deducted from the Prepaid Rent account and added to a Rent Expense account that is used in calculating net income for the year.

3. *Accrued Income*

When revenue is accrued, the business has earned the revenue by substantially completing the work, but has not yet been paid. Assume that in 1996, a company performed services for a customer and billed the customer for the agreed charge of $300, but the customer did not pay by the end of the year. Accrual means that the $300 will be recognized as revenue in 1996, so the $300 must be added to a Revenue account. The company has not received any cash, but it does have the right to receive the money, and this right is an asset. The offsetting entry is to create an asset account called Accounts Receivable, and to add the $300 to that account.

When the payment for the services is received from the customer, the business will subtract the $300 from the Accounts Receivable account and add it to the Cash account. Upon payment, the asset is no longer the right to receive the $300 (Accounts Receivable), but the actual cash itself (Cash). Revenues aren't affected by the payment because the $300 has already been recognized as revenue.

4. *Accrued Expenses*

When an expense is accrued, the business has received the economic benefit from the expense, but has not yet paid for it. For example, assume that a business rented an office in 1996, but did not pay the $7,000 bill until 1997. Accrual means that the $7,000 will be recognized as an expense in calculating 1996 income. The $7,000 is added to the Rent Expense account on the income statement. But what is the offsetting entry? The business is obligated to pay the rent; in other words, it has a liability. The $7,000 is added to a liability account with a name like Rent Expense Payable, or Rent Payable.

When the rent is eventually paid, the amount of the cash payment is deducted from the Cash account and the $7,000 is subtracted from the Rent Payable account to reflect that the liability no longer exists—it's been paid. Expenses aren't affected by the payment because the $7,000 has already been recognized as an expense.

5. *Summary*

The following table summarizes how accrual and deferral items are treated on the accounting records of the business:

ACCOUNTING TREATMENT OF DEFERRALS AND ACCRUALS

DEFERRED INCOME	*When Cash Received*	*When Recognized*
	Cash +	Revenue +
	Unearned or Deferred Revenue +	Unearned or Deferred Revenue –
DEFERRED EXPENSE	*When Cash Paid*	*When Recognized*
	Cash –	Expense +
	Prepaid or Deferred Expense +	Prepaid or Deferred Expense –
ACCRUED INCOME	*When Recognized*	*When Cash Received*
	Receivable +	Cash +
	Revenue +	Receivable –
ACCRUED EXPENSE	*When Recognized*	*When Cash Paid*
	Expense +	Cash –
	Payable +	Payable –

8

DEPRECIATION, DEPLETION AND AMORTIZATION

The Basic Concept: Allocating the Cost of Capital Assets

Many assets that a company purchases will provide benefits over several accounting periods. When a company buys a truck, it expects the truck to last for several years. The truck will help produce income throughout its life. It wouldn't be accurate to charge the entire cost of the truck as an expense in the year the truck is purchased; that's not the only income its cost will help to produce. The truck will provide benefits for several years, so the expense of buying the truck should be spread over those years.

Payments for assets like the truck that will provide benefits over more than one accounting period are called ***capital expenditures. Depreciation, depletion***, and ***amortization*** are all ways of allocating the expense of long-lived assets (capital expenditures) over some period of time, typically the expected life of the asset. When the asset is plant or equipment, the term depreciation is used. When the asset is a natural resource, like oil, gas, or timber, the term depletion is used. When the asset is an intangible, like a patent or goodwill, the term amortization is used. In spite of the different names, the basic accounting process is essentially the same: to split up the cost of the asset and allocate it as an expense over several accounting periods. The only major long-lived asset whose cost is not allocated in this way is land. The costs of structures and equipment on land are depreciated, and the costs of natural resources on land are depleted, but the cost of the land itself is not usually allocated as an expense.

The Effect of Depreciation on the Accounting Statements

Depreciation (and depletion and amortization) affect both the income statement and the balance sheet. Depreciation affects the income statement because it is an expense which reduces net income. Depreciation affects the balance sheet in two ways, one direct and one indirect. The direct effect is that depreciation reduces the accounting value of the asset being depreciated. The indirect effect of depreciation on the balance sheet results from its effect on income. Depreciation, an expense, reduces net income, and the amount of net income affects the Retained

Earnings account. Thus, depreciation indirectly reduces equity.[1]

Depreciation does not affect a company's cash flow in any way. Although depreciation is an expense, no cash payment is made for depreciation. Depreciation merely allocates as an expense the cash *previously* paid for an asset when it was acquired. Similarly, the process of depreciation provides no cash to purchase a new asset when the old one wears out. A company is not required to set aside cash as an asset is depreciated. Depreciation is only a bookkeeping entry.

Methods of Calculating Depreciation

Several different methods of calculating depreciation are acceptable. The easiest method is the **straight-line** method. Under the straight-line method, the cost of the asset is allocated equally over its useful life. For example, assume that a company pays $15,500 for a truck that it expects will last for 5 years. At the end of five years, the truck will be useless to the company, but can be sold to a junkyard for its scrap value of $500. This $500 is known as the truck's **residual or salvage value**. The salvage value is simply the value of the asset at the end of its useful life. The difference between the cost of the truck and its salvage value is known as the **depreciable cost**. The depreciable cost of the truck is $15,500 − $500 = $15,000. The straight-line method allocates the depreciable cost of the asset evenly over its useful life. Using the straight-line method, the annual depreciation will be $15,000 ÷ 5 = $3,000 each year. In other words, $1/5$ or 20% of the depreciable cost of the truck is depreciated each year. After five years, the truck is fully depreciated, and no further depreciation is taken, even if it is still in use.

Another method of depreciation, known as the **unit of output** method, allocates the cost of an asset over its useful life measured not in years, but in units of output. Consider the $15,500 truck again. The truck's useful life may depend more on how much it is driven than on the number of years the company owns it. If so, the number of miles the truck is driven is the relevant unit of output. If the useful life of the truck is 100,000 miles and its salvage value after 100,000 miles is $500, then the depreciation per mile driven is $15,000 ÷ 100,000 = $.15 per mile. Using the unit of output method, the amount of depreciation for any given year would be the number of miles the truck was driven that year multiplied by $.15 per mile. If the truck was driven 25,000 miles in one year, depreciation for that year would be 25,000 x $.15 = $3,750.

Accelerated depreciation methods take more depreciation in the early years of the asset and less in later years. The two primary acceler-

---

[1] And, since you're subtracting the same amount from each side of the balance sheet, it continues to balance. Accountants are such miracle workers!

ated depreciation methods are the ***double-declining-balance*** method and the ***sum-of-the-years'-digits*** method. In the ***double-declining-balance*** method, the normal, straight-line rate of depreciation is doubled and the doubled rate is applied each year to the *book value* of the asset.[2] Assume again that a company pays $15,500 for a truck with a useful life of 5 years. As we explained previously, the straight-line method would depreciate 20% of the $15,000 depreciable cost each year. The double declining-balance method doubles this rate to 40% and deducts each year 40% of the asset's book value at the beginning of that year. The depreciation rate is applied to the full purchase price of the truck; the salvage value is not deducted. Depreciation of the truck for the first year would be $15,500 x .40 = $6,200. The book value of the truck at the end of the first year would be $15,500 - $6,200 = $9,300. Depreciation for the second year would be $9,300 x .40 = $3,720. The book value of the truck at the end of the second year would be $9,300 - $3,720 = $5,580. Depreciation of the truck would continue at the same 40% rate as long as the truck remains in use.

The ***sum-of-the-years'-digits*** method is more complicated. The depreciation rate is a fraction. The numerator of the fraction (that's the top part) is the number of years of useful life remaining at the *beginning* of the year. The denominator of the fraction (that's the bottom part) is the sum of the years of useful life. To return to our truck example, the numerator for the first year's depreciation would be 5, since, at the beginning of the first year, when the truck is first acquired, the truck has 5 years of expected useful life. The denominator of the fraction is the sum of the five years, $1 + 2 + 3 + 4 + 5 = 15$. The fractional rate is applied to the depreciable cost of the asset. Thus, depreciation in the first year would be $5/15$, or one-third, of the $15,000 depreciable cost, which is $5,000. Depreciation in the second year would be $4/15$ of the $15,000 cost, which is $4,000. Depreciation would be $3/15$ of the $15,000 in the third year, $2/15$ in the fourth year, and $1/15$ in the fifth and final year. After five years, the truck is fully depreciated and no further depreciation is taken.

Balance Sheet Treatment of Depreciation

It is customary to show on the balance sheet the original cost of an asset, the total amount of depreciation allocated to it over the years, and the difference between the two. The original cost of an asset is known as its ***basis***. The cumulative amount of depreciation is known

---

[2] Notice that this depreciation rate is applied to the full book value of the truck; its salvage value is not subtracted. Salvage value is ignored when using the double-declining-balance method.

as **accumulated depreciation**. The difference between the original cost of an asset and its accumulated depreciation is known as the asset's **book value**. Assume that a company bought some equipment two years ago for $30,000. The useful life of the equipment is 20 years and it has no salvage value. If the company is using the straight-line method of depreciation, annual depreciation is $30,000 divided by 20, or $1,500 a year. After two years, the Equipment entry on the balance sheet would look like this:

Equipment	$30,000	
Less: Accumulated Depreciation	(3,000)	$27,000

The original cost of the equipment was $30,000. After two years, the accumulated depreciation is $3,000 ($1,500 x 2 years). The book value is the difference between these two figures, $27,000. The book value is used to total the assets on the left-hand side of the balance sheet.

Book Value and Market Value

Depreciation, depletion, and amortization spread the cost of an asset over its useful life. They do not necessarily reflect the actual deterioration of the asset or an actual decline in its market value. The horse-drawn buggy the company bought in 1880 may be fully depreciated, but it is not necessarily worthless. It may be an extremely valuable antique. The computer the company bought two years ago may not be worth as much as shown on the company's balance sheet, because of all the technological changes since then. Or, because of inflation, an asset may have a market value greater than that shown on the balance sheet because all prices have risen since it was purchased. This is one of the most important lessons of accounting: the balance sheet, or book, value of an asset is not necessarily its market value.

Depletion of Natural Resources

Depletion is the equivalent of depreciation when the asset is a natural resource, like mineral deposits or oil and gas. Depletion is measured by dividing the cost of the natural resource by the total number of available units. Assume, for example, that a company pays $5 million for the oil rights on property estimated to contain 1 million barrels of oil. The cost per barrel is $5 million divided by 1 million barrels, or $5. If the company extracts and sells 150,000 barrels in the first year, the amount of depletion is $5 per barrel times 150,000 barrels, or $750,000. Depletion, like depreciation, is an expense to be deducted from revenue in calculating net income. Depletion also affects the balance sheet in the same way as depreciation. The original cost of the asset (Oil Reserves in the example) must be reduced on the balance sheet by the amount of the accumulated depletion. After the first year's depletion, the entry for Oil Reserves on the asset side of the balance sheet would look like this:

Oil Reserves	$5,000,000	
Less: Accumulated Depletion	(750,000)	$4,250,000

Amortization of Intangibles

Amortization is the same concept applied to intangible assets like patents, trademarks, leaseholds, and goodwill. Amortization allocates the cost of an intangible asset over its useful life. Assume, for example, that a company purchases a patent from an inventor for $400,000. It expects the patent to have economic value for 10 years, after which the invention will become obsolete and be of no further value to the company. Intangible assets are usually amortized using the straight-line method. Each year, the company will recognize an amortization expense of $40,000 ($400,000 ÷ 10) and reduce the balance sheet value of the patent by $40,000. The usual accounting practice is not to use an "Accumulated Amortization" account. The value of the patent on the balance sheet is simply reduced by the amount of the amortization, without any offsetting accumulated amortization account.

Changes in Depreciation

Obviously, the calculation of depreciation is subject to judgment and error. The method of depreciation chosen will affect the amount of depreciation each year. Also, both the useful life of an asset and its salvage value are estimates. Variations in the estimates will affect the amount of depreciation each year.

What happens if it becomes obvious that one of those estimates is wrong? For example, assume that a company buys a computer for $5,000. To make the example simple, assume that the computer has no salvage value; after its useful life, it will be worthless. The company estimates a useful life of 10 years and begins depreciating the computer at the rate of $500 a year. After two years, when the book value of the computer is $4,000, the company decides that, because of rapid advances in software and computer peripherals, the computer's useful life will only be a total of four years. Two years from now, the computer will be worthless.[3] What should the company do?

---

[3] Does this sound familiar to those of you who have purchased computers in the last ten years?

Past depreciation is not affected; no retroactive changes are made. The $500 depreciation expense for each of the past two years is not changed and the accumulated depreciation of $1,000 stays the same. However, the company must adjust future depreciation of the computer to match the new estimate of useful life. The remaining book value must be spread over the shorter useful life. The book value is $4,000 and the remaining useful life is 2 years, so, using the straight-line method, the depreciation expense for each of the next two years is $2,000.

What if the company makes an expenditure that will increase the useful life of the asset? To understand the answer to this question, we need to distinguish between **capital expenditures** and **revenue expenditures**. A **capital expenditure** is any expenditure that will benefit several accounting periods. A **revenue expenditure** is an expenditure that benefits only the current accounting period. The cost of ordinary maintenance and repair of an asset is a revenue expenditure. If the asset is a truck, for example, the costs of oil, gas, and routine maintenance are revenue expenditures. Such expenses are sometimes called **ordinary repairs**. Ordinary repairs also include the cost of relatively small components of the asset—such as tires or spark plugs in the truck. These components will probably last for more than one accounting period, but, as a practical matter, small expenses like this aren't depreciated.

However, certain additions or improvements to assets are so significant that they are treated as capital expenditures. If the company replaces the engine of its truck with a completely new engine, that is probably a capital expenditure. If the company adds a new addition to its existing building, that is a capital expenditure. The difference between an ordinary repair and a capital expenditure is one of degree, requiring some accounting judgment.[4]

Capital additions or improvements to an existing asset increase the book value (and perhaps the useful life) of the asset. Assume, for example, that the company bought a truck for $15,500 four years ago. The truck's expected useful life is five years and its salvage value is $500. After four years, using the straight-line method of depreciation, accumulated depreciation is $12,000 ($3,000 per year times 4 years). The book value of the truck after four years is $3,500. Assume the company pays $5,000 to put a new engine in the truck. With the new engine, the truck will be useful to the company for another four years (three years beyond the original expected useful life). The cost of the engine is a capital expenditure. Its effect is to increase the depreciable cost of the truck by $5,000 and to extend its useful life by three years. This change is treated

---

[4] The lawyer author thinks "accounting judgment" is probably an oxymoron, like "military intelligence" and "political insight."

essentially the same as if the company's estimates of useful life or salvage value changed. No retroactive changes are made to the company's accounting statements, but the new numbers must be used in calculating future depreciation. The total depreciable cost of the truck is now $3,500 + $5,000 - $500 = $8,000 (assuming that the installation of the new engine has not affected the truck's salvage value). Its remaining useful life is now four more years. The depreciation expense for each of the next four years, using a straight-line method, is $8,000 ÷ 4 = $2,000 each year.

9

INVENTORY

Introduction

You probably have heard the phrase "taking inventory," as in, "I'm taking inventory of all the reasons why I shouldn't have come to law school." **Inventory** is the accounting term for the goods a business holds for sale to its customers in the regular course of business.[1] If the company is only a merchandising company (meaning that it sells goods manufactured by others), inventory is the goods available to be sold to customers. When you walk into a department store, all of the items for sale on the shelves are inventory, plus any merchandise the store has stored in the back or in a separate warehouse.[2]

If the company is a manufacturing company (meaning that it manufactures its own goods for sale), inventory includes more. A manufacturing company has three types of inventory: (1) *raw materials*, (2) *work in process*, and (3) *finished goods*. *Raw materials* are the materials used to make the goods which the company manufactures. For example, if the company makes steel, the raw materials are the coal, iron, and Acme Instant Steel Mix that the company uses to make the steel.[3] *Work in process* is unfinished goods that the company has begun to make but not yet completed. For example, if the steel company has combined the coal, iron, and Instant Steel Mix in its giant mixing bowl, but it has not yet hardened, this would be work in process. *Finished goods* are the completed goods, ready for sale; in the case of the steel company, this would be the finished steel.

Beginning and Ending Inventory and the Cost of Goods Sold

A company's inventory changes during each accounting period. Unless the company is a total failure, it sells some of its inventory to

---

[1] To put it more technically, inventory is the stuff sitting around waiting to be sold.

[2] To impress others with your new accounting sophistication, walk into a busy store and, in your loudest voice, exclaim, "Wow! Look at all this inventory."

[3] Even we realize that steel isn't made with something called Acme Instant Steel Mix. How stupid do you think we are? The Japanese drove most American companies, including Acme, out of business in the 1980's. Most steel manufacturers now use Nokamura Instant Steel Mix.

customers. That is, after all, why it was holding the inventory in the first place. These sales reduce its inventory. The company may also add to its inventory by purchasing more goods to sell or, if it's a manufacturing company, by making more goods to sell.

Beginning Inventory is the inventory on hand for sale at the beginning of an accounting period. *Ending Inventory* is the inventory on hand at the end of an accounting period. The basic inventory equation is:

Beginning   +   Inventory Purchased   –   Cost of   =   Ending
Inventory   or Manufactured   Goods Sold   Inventory

The accounting value of the inventory at the end of the period (Ending Inventory) is equal to the value of the inventory at the beginning of the period (Beginning Inventory) plus additions to that inventory (Inventory Purchased or Manufactured) minus what was sold (Cost of Goods Sold).[4]

Using a little algebra,[5] this equation becomes:

Cost of   =   Beginning   +   Inventory Purchased   –   Ending
Goods Sold   Inventory   or Manufactured   Inventory

To compute the cost of the goods that have been sold during the period (the Cost of Goods Sold), you look at how much you had at the beginning of the period (Beginning Inventory) and how much you added during the period (Inventory Purchased or Manufactured), and compare that to what's left at the end of the period (Ending Inventory). Ignoring the problem of theft, the difference is what you sold.

The *Cost of Goods Sold*—the inventory sold during the period—is an expense. Selling those goods produced revenue and the cost of the goods must be subtracted from that revenue to determine the net income or loss arising from the sales.

To use the inventory equation, the company must know its opening and closing inventories. Companies keep track of inventory in two ways. One method is the *periodic method*. Under the periodic method, a physical count of the company's inventory is done periodically; this count is known as taking inventory. The second method is the *perpetual method*, where the company keeps a running tab of inventory. Additions to inventory are made on the company's records as goods come in and deductions are made on the company's records as goods are sold. A single business may use both methods—keeping a tab on an ongoing,

---

[4] In more technical accounting lingo, the stuff you have at the end of the year is what you had to start with plus new stuff minus stuff you sold. Only an accounting professional could have figured this one out.

[5] We won't bore you with the algebra because, frankly, we're not very good at it.

perpetual basis, with a periodic check to verify that the running tab is accurate.

Inventory on the Balance Sheet

Inventory is an asset. Like most other assets, it is usually valued on the balance sheet at its cost to the business. The cost of the inventory is the sum of all the expenditures and charges directly or indirectly incurred in bringing the inventory to its present condition and location. If the company is a merchandising company that buys its goods from someone else, the cost is the price it paid for the goods, including any transportation costs it had to pay. If the company is a manufacturing company that makes the goods it sells, the cost is the cost of manufacturing the goods, including the cost of all the raw materials.

Unlike some other assets, however, inventory is sometimes properly valued at less than its cost. To value inventory on the balance sheet, accountants apply a difficult rule known as the ***lower-of-cost-or-market rule***. This rule applies whenever, because of physical damage, deterioration, obsolescence, or a decline in prices, the cost of the goods in inventory has declined since the company acquired them. "Market" in this rule usually means not the price at which the company can sell the goods, but their ***replacement cost***—what it would cost the company at today's prices to purchase or produce the inventory. The lower-of-cost-or-market rule says that, if the replacement cost of the inventory is less than its actual cost, the closing inventory value on the balance sheet should be reduced to the market cost—the replacement cost. You use the lower of the two values, cost or replacement cost.

For example, if the Ma Yo-Yo Store bought its yo-yos from the manufacturer for $5 each, but the manufacturer is now selling them for $4, the book value of the yo-yos would have to be reduced to $4 each. A couple of exceptions you don't want to know about complicate this rule,[6] but the basic point is that the book value of inventory will sometimes be less than what the company paid for it. If the book value of inventory is reduced using the lower-of-cost-or-market rule, the amount of the reduction is either treated as an addition to the Cost of Goods Sold for that period or shown separately as a loss on the income statement.

It is important to understand that the lower-of-cost-or-market rule only applies if the market value is below the cost—what the business paid for the inventory. The lower-of-cost-or-market rule requires a company to reduce the book value of its inventory below the inventory's cost; it does not allow a company to increase the book value of its

---

[6] If you must know, the "market" figure cannot exceed net realizable value and cannot be less than net realizable value less normal profit. We told you you didn't want to know.

inventory above its actual cost if the replacement cost is higher. Valuing inventory on the balance sheet above its cost is usually unacceptable.

Inventory as an Expense: The Cost of Goods Sold

The Cost of Goods Sold is an expense. When a company sells some of its inventory, it receives revenue. The Cost of Goods Sold is one of the expenses associated with that revenue. Unfortunately, it is not always easy to determine the Cost of Goods Sold. The cost of manufacturing or purchasing inventory often varies over time. When some of the inventory is sold, which of the various possible costs should be used? For example, assume that Acme Corporation sells widgets,[7] all of which are identical. Acme bought the widgets it owns over a period of several years, at prices ranging from $3 to $6 per widget. When Acme sells one particular widget, what is the cost of the widget it sold? Which cost in the $3 to $6 range it paid is its expense?

Several different methods of computing the Cost of Goods Sold are acceptable to accountants. One possibility is what's known as **specific identification**. Acme could keep track of each individual widget and what it cost. It might, for example, put a number on each widget when it buys it that indicates how much Acme paid for it. When Acme sells a widget, it could look at the number on the particular widget to see how much it cost and use that cost as the Cost of Goods Sold. Specific identification makes sense for some types of goods—particularly goods that are unique and very valuable. An art dealer should keep a record of each valuable painting purchased and, when it is sold, match that expense to the sale. But specific identification doesn't make much sense for goods like widgets that are low cost and fungible. Acme doesn't want to keep track of the specific cost of each widget; it may have thousands or even millions of them.[8] Some other method is needed.

Three other methods are commonly used: the **FIFO method**, the **LIFO method**, and the **average cost method**. The **FIFO (First In, First Out) method** assumes that goods are sold in the order in which the business originally purchased them. The first units of inventory purchased—the ones the business has held the longest—are assumed to be the first ones sold. To determine the cost of goods sold, you begin

---

[7] Business and accounting professors always hypothesize that companies sell widgets. No one knows what a widget is. Our dictionary, for example, defines it as a "hypothetical manufactured article." THE AMERICAN HERITAGE DICTIONARY OF THE ENGLISH LANGUAGE 2040 (3d ed. 1992). As far as we know, you can only buy them in hypothetical stores. Business and accounting professors use widgets as an example because, most of them, like many law professors, have no idea what businesses actually sell. We don't either, so we'll stick with widgets.

[8] Hard to say, since we don't know what they are.

with the cost of the oldest unit in inventory, continue to the next oldest unit, and so on, until the total amount sold has been reached.

The **LIFO (Last In, First Out) method** assumes that the goods are sold in exactly the opposite of the order in which the business originally purchased them. The units purchased most recently—the ones the business has held the shortest amount of time—are assumed to be the first ones sold. To determine the cost of goods sold, you begin with the cost of the newest unit in inventory, continue to the next most recent unit, and so on, until the total amount sold has been reached.

The **average cost method** averages the costs of all the units in inventory. The total cost basis of the inventory is divided by the total number of units to produce an average cost per unit. To determine the cost of goods sold, you multiply this average cost by the number of units sold.

An example will illustrate the differences among the FIFO, LIFO, and average cost methods. Assume that Acme's beginning inventory is 100 widgets. Ten of those widgets were acquired in 1993 for $3 each; 30 of those widgets were acquired in 1994 for $4 each; 25 of those widgets were acquired in 1995 for $5 each; and the remaining 35 widgets were acquired in 1996 for $6 each. The following table summarizes these figures:

Year	1993	1994	1995	1996
No. of widgets	10	30	25	35
Cost	$3	$4	$5	$6

The total book value of the widgets is $485 [(10 x $3) + (30 x $4) + (25 x $5) + (35 x $6)]. Assume that, in 1997, Acme sells 62 widgets and does not buy any more widgets. Using each method, what will the cost of goods sold be and what will the book value of ending inventory be?

The LIFO method assumes that the 62 most recently acquired widgets are the ones that are sold—the 35 that were purchased in 1996, the 25 that were purchased in 1995, and 2 of the 30 that were purchased in 1994. The Cost of Goods Sold is $343 [(35 x $6) + (25 x $5) + (2 x $4)]. The book value of the ending inventory, the difference between the beginning inventory and the cost of goods sold, is $485 - $343 = $142.

The FIFO method assumes that the 62 units sold are the oldest ones in inventory—the 10 that were purchased in 1993, the 30 that were purchased in 1994, and 22 of the 25 that were purchased in 1995. The Cost of Goods Sold is $260 [(10 x $3) + (30 x $4) + (22 x $5)]. The value of the ending inventory, the difference between beginning inventory and the cost of goods sold, is $485 - $260 = $225.

The average cost method uses average values. The average cost of each widget in inventory is $4.85, the total cost of the inventory, $485, divided by the total number of widgets, 100. The Cost of Goods Sold is this average cost times the number of widgets sold, $4.85 x 62 = $300.70. The value of the ending inventory is the difference between beginning inventory and the cost of goods sold, $485 - $300.70 = $184.30.

The inventory method chosen affects both income and the valuation of inventory on the balance sheet. If costs are rising (an inflationary economy), then inventory purchased more recently cost more than older inventory. In that case, the LIFO method produces a higher Cost of Goods Sold and a lower income than the FIFO method. Since the Closing Inventory on the balance sheet is the inventory remaining unsold, the LIFO method results in a lower inventory value on the balance sheet than the FIFO method. If costs are falling (an imaginary economy), then inventory purchased more recently cost less than older inventory. In that case, the LIFO method produces a lower Cost of Goods Sold, a higher income, and a higher inventory value on the balance sheet than the FIFO method.

10

CONTINGENCIES

An interesting[1] accrual problem is what to do about contingencies—losses or gains that may or may not materialize sometime in the future. For example, assume that a customer sued a company in 1996 for $100,000 alleging that a product the customer purchased is defective. The lawsuit has not yet been tried. This is a **contingent loss** to the business—whether the company has to pay the $100,000 depends on the outcome of the litigation. It is a **contingent gain** to the customer—whether the customer receives the $100,000 depends on the outcome of the litigation. Should this potential liability be accrued and reflected in the accounting statements now in spite of its uncertainty or should the company wait until the case is decided?

Accountants are somewhat inconsistent in their treatment of contingent gains and losses, and the inconsistency relates to their gloomy nature, which accountants call **conservatism**. As a general rule, accountants believe in painting as negative a picture as possible. Thus, the following rules: Contingent *gains* are almost never recognized. The customer will not recognize any of the potential gain from the lawsuit until the litigation is concluded. But *loss* contingencies must be accrued and reflected on the accounting statements if two conditions are met: (1) it is probable that a loss will occur in the future, and (2) the amount of the loss can be reasonably estimated. If these conditions are met, the company has to include the estimated amount of the loss on its financial statements for 1996, even though the case has not yet been decided.

If the loss contingency is accrued and recognized, the probable amount of the loss is treated as a current expense, charged against income for the period. The offsetting entry to make the accounts balance is to create a liability with a name like Contingent Liability. Thus, if the company believes that it will lose the lawsuit and its estimated damages are $85,000, it will add an $85,000 Litigation Expense to the Income Statement and create an $85,000 liability with a name like Contingent

---

[1] "Interesting" may be too strong a word. Accountants think it's interesting, but accountants are also mesmerized by the question of whether their socks should match their pants or their shirt.

Litigation Liability. If the contingency eventually occurs (the company loses the lawsuit), the contingent liability account is eliminated and the Cash account reduced by the amount paid. If the company gets lucky and the contingency does not occur (the company wins the lawsuit), the contingent liability account is still eliminated. However, the offsetting entry is to reduce the expense for the current period, to make up for the amount that was previously charged against income but never incurred.

If the company decides that the contingent loss is not probable or the amount of the loss can't be estimated, it does not have to accrue the liability. However, it still must disclose the contingent liability in a footnote to its financial statements if there is at least a reasonable possibility that a material loss may occur.

A company sometimes has a group of related contingencies. A company that sells its products on credit has many accounts receivable, some of which may not be paid. A company that sells consumer products may face a large number of warranty or product defect claims, only some of which it will lose. The company may not know whether any particular one of those individual claims will succeed, but it may be able to estimate, based on past experience, that a certain percentage of all the warranty claims will be successful or that a certain percentage of all the accounts receivable will be uncollectible. Considering each individual claim alone, the two-part test for recognizing a loss contingency is not met. The company cannot say whether a loss is probable. However, considering all of the claims as a group, the company can say that a loss is probable and can reasonably estimate its amount, because it can estimate the overall percentage of claims that will succeed. If this is the case, the company must accrue the expected amount of the loss on a group basis, in the same way that it would accrue an individual loss contingency. In the accounts receivable example, it would add the probable amount of the loss to an account called something like Allowance for Uncollectible Accounts and the offsetting entry would be an Uncollectible Accounts Expense on the income statement. It is customary to show the Allowance for Uncollectible Accounts as an offset to Accounts Receivable on the asset side of the balance sheet. For example, if the company has Accounts Receivable of $150,000 and estimates that ten percent of that amount is uncollectible, that portion of the assets section of the balance sheet would look like this:

Accounts Receivable	$150,000	
Less: Allowance for Uncollectible Accounts	(15,000)	$135,000

Even if a company is not required to accrue a contingent loss and treat it as a current expense, it may still want its balance sheet to show the contingency. This is sometimes done by creating a reserve account in the equity section of the balance sheet. Recall that the equity or net worth section of the balance sheet represents the net worth of the business—the residual difference between assets and liabilities. If the contingency materializes, it will reduce the net worth of the business. It is therefore customary to record such a reserve account as a separate part of the equity section of the balance sheet, indicating that there is no liability yet but, if the contingency occurs, the equity of the business will be reduced by the amount of the reserve. The Retained Earnings account is reduced by the amount the company intends to record for the contingency; that amount is then moved into another equity account with a title like Provision for Contingencies or Reserve for Litigation Contingency. Since you're simply reallocating amounts from one equity account to another, the Asset and Liability sections are unaffected. The creation of this Reserve or Contingency account does not mean that any money or other property has been set aside to pay the contingency if it materializes. This is purely an accounting change.

If the contingency materializes and the business suffers a loss, the reserve account is eliminated and the loss charged against net income as an expense. If the contingency does not materialize, the reserve account is eliminated and the amount of the reserve is returned to the retained earnings account.

11

CASH FLOW: THE STATEMENT OF CASH FLOWS

In 1993, IBM posted a record loss for the year of more than $8 billion dollars, its third consecutive annual net loss of more than a billion dollars. Yet IBM remained in business. IBM is not alone; other companies have had large operating losses for several consecutive years and still continued to operate. On the other hand, many companies with consistently good net incomes have difficulty continuing in business. For example, in 1989, Prime Motor Inns, the second largest hotel operator in the world, had revenues of $410 million and a net income of $77 million. Its 1989 revenues were almost 11 percent greater than its 1988 revenues. In spite of this impressive showing, Prime Motor Inns filed for bankruptcy the following September.[1] What explains this discrepancy between a company's income or losses and its ability to remain in business? The answer lies, at least in part, in *cash flows*.

IBM and other companies which continue in business despite massive losses either have sufficient cash reserves (savings) to weather the problems or they can obtain cash by selling assets and stock or borrowing money. Companies like Prime Motor Inns may be profitable, but their profits are tied up in assets other than cash. Unfortunately, you can't pay creditors and employees with buildings, equipment, or inventory. Without cash to pay bills, a company can be forced into bankruptcy.

The experiences of many law students also illustrate why cash flows, and not just net income, are important. During law school, you are probably operating at a net loss. Your expenses—what you're paying for food, rent, tuition, and so forth—are greater than your income from your work and any investments you might have. How are you able to continue in law school in spite of this loss? You have additional cash available— savings you set aside in the past, loans, or scholarships. Even though you have a net operating loss, you have sufficient cash (barely) to pay your bills.

Let's consider your *cash flow*—where your cash comes from and where it goes. If you were to list the sources of cash you receive, your list would probably look something like the following:

---

[1] "Lies of the Bottom Line," Forbes (November 12, 1990).

1. Money from a part-time job.
2. Student loans.
3. Loans from parents.
4. Grants from government agencies.
5. Scholarships.
6. Gifts from parents, grandparents, and others.
7. Sales of assets you own, such as your car, your coin collection, stock, etc.

If you listed how you spend your cash, you might come up with a list that looks like the following:

1. Rent and other bills.
2. Food and entertainment.
3. Tuition.
4. Books.
5. Taxes.
6. Interest.
7. Repayment of loans.
8. Automobile.
9. Bribes to professors for good grades.[2]

You may have other sources of cash and you may spend your cash in other ways, but these lists are complete enough to demonstrate the concept. Let's classify the ways that you obtain and spend cash into three categories: 1) cash flows from operations (i.e., jobs and ordinary day-to-day living expenses), 2) cash flows from investing activities, and 3) cash flows from financing activities:

Cash Flows From Operations:
    Cash received from job
    Cash used to pay rent and other bills
    Cash used to pay tuition
    Cash used to buy books
    Cash used to pay taxes
    Cash used to pay interest
    Cash used to bribe professors

Cash Flows From Investing Activities:
    Cash from the sale of assets such as car, coin collection, etc.

---

[2] The authors wish to inform their students that this last item is only a joke, and that cash may be forwarded to Account 51C37S4 at the National Bank of Switzerland.

Cash paid to purchase automobile

Cash Flows From Financing Activities:

Cash from student loans

Cash loans from parents

Cash from grants from government agencies

Cash from scholarships

Cash gifts from parents, grandparents, and others

Cash used to repay loans

Some of these activities increase your cash and some of these activities decrease your cash. The net difference between the cash coming in and the cash going out is known as your cash flow. If you're taking in more cash than you're spending, your cash flow is positive. If you're spending more cash than you're taking in, your cash flow is negative.

Businesses receive and disburse cash in much the same ways and for the same types of purposes as law students. A company's **operating activities** are the transactions associated with its sales of goods and services—cash received from sales and the cash paid for expenses to produce those sales. Cash flow from a company's **investing activities** results from the cash the company pays to acquire investments or long-lived, capital assets, the cash it receives as a return on those investments, and the cash it receives from selling those investments and capital assets. A company's **financing activities** relate to its liabilities and equity accounts—the cash received by borrowing money, the cash received from investors (as when a corporation sells stock), and the cash paid out to investors (as when a corporation pays dividends to its stockholders).

The **Statement of Cash Flows**, which replaced a statement called the **Statement of Changes in Financial Position**, is an accounting statement that tracks a company's or individual's cash flow for a specified period. It shows how much cash the company had at the start of the period, the amount of cash it received during the period, the amount of cash it paid out during the period, and how much cash the company had at the end of the period. The relationship between these different amounts is fairly simple:

Cash, Beginning   +   Cash   –   Cash   =   Cash, End
of Period   Coming In   Going Out   of Period

The Statement of Cash Flows may be prepared in one of two different ways: the **Direct Method** or the **Indirect Method**.[3] Both methods should end up with the same cash flow; they just get there in different ways.

---

[3] The names of the methods are not very exciting, but what do you expect from accountants?

The difference between them is in how they determine Cash Flows From Operations. Cash Flows from Investing Activities and Cash Flows from Financing Activities are the same under both methods.

The **Direct Method** looks to each of the various accounts and asks how much cash was paid or received in connection with each account during the period. How much of the company's revenues were received in cash in the period? How much cash was received for accounts receivable during the period? How much cash did the company pay for various expenses during the period? How much cash did the company pay to buy assets during the period? How much cash was received for selling assets during the period? How much cash was received for liabilities the company incurred? How much cash was used to pay off liabilities?

The **Indirect Method** uses Net Income for the period as a starting point. For instance, assume that a company has Total Revenues for the year of $300,000 and Total Expenses of $250,000. Its Net Income is $50,000. Assume that all revenues were received in cash, so no adjustments need to be made to revenues. But one of the expenses was depreciation, in the amount of $5,000. Depreciation expense reduced the company's net income by $5,000, but no cash is paid out for depreciation. It's merely a bookkeeping entry. The company's net cash flow was actually $5,000 greater than its net income, so we have to add the $5,000 back in to determine the company's net cash flow, $55,000.

Let's consider a more detailed example. Assume that Acme Company's balance sheets for 1995 and 1996 look like this:

Acme Corporation
Balance Sheets
For the Years 1995 and 1996

1995

Assets		Liabilities and Equity	
Cash	$4,600	Accounts Payable	$ 600
Supplies	500	Long-term Debt	500
Equipment	0	Stockholders' Equity	4,000
Total Assets	$5,100	Total	$5,100

1996

Assets			Liabilities	
Cash		$5,000	Accounts Payable	$ 800
Supplies		600	Long-term Debt	0
Equipment	$2,500		Stockholders' Equity	6,800
Less:Accum Deprec. 500	2,000			
Total Assets	$7,600		Total	$7,600

The company's income statement for 1996 looks like this:

Acme Corporation
Income Statement
1996

Sales Revenue		$ 46,000
Expenses:		
Wages	$ 32,000	
Supplies	5,200	
Depreciation	500	
Total Expenses		37,700
Net Income		$ 8,300

Acme's net cash flow during 1996 is obvious from the two balance sheets. All you have to do is compare the Cash accounts. At the end of 1995, Acme had $4,600 cash. At the end of 1996, it had $5,000 cash. Its net cash flow during 1996 was an increase of $400. But, if Acme had a net income of $8,300 in 1996, why did its cash only increase by $400? To see what happened, let's prepare a Statement of Cash Flows for Acme. If we use the indirect method, Acme's Statement of Cash Flows for 1996 would look like this:

Acme Corporation
Statement of Cash Flows
1996

Cash Flows From Operating Activities		
Net Income	$ 8,300	
Adjustments to reconcile net income to cash provided by operations:		
Increase in Supplies	(100)	
Increase in Accounts Payable	200	
Depreciation Expense	500	
Cash Provided by Operating Activities		$8,900
Cash Flows From Investing Activities		
Purchase of Equipment		(2,500)
Cash Flows From Financing Activities		
Retirement of long-term debt	$ (500)	
Sale of Stock	1,000	
Payment of Dividends	(6,500)	
Total Cash Flows From Investing Activities		(6,000)
Total Increase in Cash		$ 400
Cash, December 31, 1995		4,600
Cash, December 31, 1996		$5,000

We start with the company's net income, $8,300. To determine cash flow, we must make several adjustments to net income. We must subtract all the cash payments the company made that were not treated as current expenses and therefore did not affect net income. We must add back all of the cash receipts the company had that were not treated as revenues and therefore did not affect net income. We must remove any expenses or revenues that were accrued, where no cash has yet changed hands. And we must add in any expenses or revenues that were deferred, where cash has been paid, but not yet charged to income. What's left after we make all of these adjustments should be the company's net cash flow.

Even in this simple example, the difference between net income and cash flow is not quickly explained. Cash From Operations increased not just by the $8,300 of net income but by $8,900. Three adjustments are necessary. First, the company increased its inventory of Supplies, using cash to purchase a non-cash asset which didn't affect net income. Second, the company delayed paying some legitimate debts (Accounts Payable) and saved the cash, even though the debts were treated as expenses to calculate net income. Third, the company had an expense (Depreciation) for which no cash was paid.

Look now at cash flows from investing activities. The company used $2,500 of its cash to purchase new equipment, which is an investing activity. Except for the $500 that was depreciated in 1996, this is not an expense, so it did not reduce net income. Turn now to financing activities. Five hundred dollars of the remaining difference is due to the retirement of debt—the company used $500 cash to pay off its long-term debt. The company sold stock for $1,000, increasing its cash by $1,000. But it paid cash dividends of $6,500, reducing its cash by $6,500.

When we add and subtract all of these adjustments, the company's net cash flow is a $400 gain, the difference between the Cash accounts on the two balance sheets.

SECTION FOUR:

THE ACCOUNTING
ENVIRONMENT

12

GENERALLY ACCEPTED ACCOUNTING PRINCIPLES

This book explains many accounting principles: how to prepare financial statements, how to record various types of transactions on a company's accounting records, the basic rules of accounting. But where do those rules come from and how do accountants know what they are? What keeps accountants from just making up numbers that have no relationship to reality?[1] If you like acronyms, consider the following sentence: Accountants follow GAAP, which are derived from the FASB, the EITF, the AICPA Ac-SEC and ASB, SEC FRRs (formerly ASRs) and SABs, the AICPA CAP, the APB, and even the IRS. When the professor calls on you, try that line. If you're afraid of what your professor would do to you,[2] and you want to know what all this means, read on.

Accountants prepare financial statements and accounting records in accordance with what are known as *generally accepted accounting principles*, commonly abbreviated as *GAAP*.[3] Generally accepted accounting principles are not contained in a single, codified set of rules. They consist of the accepted practices of the accounting profession, as set forth in a variety of publications and as actually practiced by reputable accountants.

Generally accepted accounting principles vary substantially from country to country. For example, when Daimler-Benz, a German company, prepared financial statements in accordance with U.S. GAAP, it had a $1 billion loss for the year. Under German accounting principles,

---

[1] The accountant author of this book believes that, even without rules, accountants wouldn't prepare misleading financial statements because accountants are all honest, decent, upright, principled human beings. The lawyer author of this book believes the accountant author is losing touch with reality.

[2] The law professor author of this book believes no law student would be afraid of a law professor. Law professors are all warm, friendly, gentle human beings with great senses of humor. The accountant author believes the law professor author is losing touch with reality.

[3] This acronym is pronounced "gap," like the jeans store and the space between David Letterman's front teeth.

it had a $100 million profit.[4] It's hard enough to learn one set of accounting principles, so we'll focus on the American rules.[5]

The Financial Accounting Standards Board (FASB)

The leading source of GAAP is the **Financial Accounting Standards Board**, usually known by the acronym **FASB**.[6] FASB is an independent body with seven full-time members which issues several types of releases on accounting issues.[7] The most important and authoritative are **Statements of Financial Accounting Standards (SFAS)**, which establish new accounting standards or principles. The FASB also issues **Interpretations**, which explain or clarify existing accounting standards, and **Statements of Financial Accounting Concepts**, which don't contain new standards or principles, but provide problem-solving guidance to accountants. The FASB staff also issues **Technical Bulletins** to provide guidance in individual cases.

Why are the FASB's pronouncements followed by the accounting profession? One answer lies in the Code of Professional Conduct of the **American Institute of Certified Public Accountants (AICPA)**, the national professional association of certified public accountants.[8] A **certified public accountant**, or **CPA**, is a state-certified professional who offers accounting services to clients for a fee. In essence, CPAs are the accounting equivalent of lawyers engaged in private practice. Rule 203 of the AICPA Code of Professional Conduct prohibits CPAs from giving an opinion that financial statements are in accord with generally accepted accounting principles if those statements depart from the FASB principles and the departure materially affects the financial statements taken as a whole.[9]

The FASB's position is buttressed by the position of the **Securities and Exchange Commission (SEC)**, the agency which administers the federal securities laws. Since 1938, the SEC has indicated that financial statements prepared in accordance with accounting principles without "substantial authoritative support" are presumed misleading.[10] Princi-

---

[4] Lee Berton, "All Accountants Soon May Speak the Same Language," WALL ST. J., Aug. 29, 1995.

[5] The fact that neither of the authors knows the German rules has nothing to do with it.

[6] This is pronounced faz bee.

[7] FASB has a counterpart, the Governmental Accounting Standards Board (GASB), that establishes accounting principles for state and local governments.

[8] For more on CPAs, see the discussion of auditing in Chapter 15.

[9] Rule 203 allows a departure from FASB principles if the auditor believes that compliance with FASB principles would render the financial statements misleading. However, this exception is rarely invoked.

[10] Accounting Series Release No. 4; Financial Reporting Release No. 1 § 101.

ples, standards, and practices promulgated by the FASB (and its predecessors) are deemed to have substantial authoritative support. Accounting principles contrary to FASB standards are considered *not* to have substantial authoritative support, and are therefore presumed to be misleading. The SEC position essentially gives accountants and their clients a choice between following the FASB rules or committing federal securities fraud.

Emerging Issues Task Force (EITF)

The FASB operates at a rather slow, perhaps even glacial, pace. The FASB's procedures are cumbersome and loaded with due process protections, and it sometimes takes several years to address major issues. In 1984, the FASB established an **Emerging Issues Task Force (EITF)**, which deals with cutting-edge accounting issues and generally operates more swiftly than the FASB itself.

The Securities and Exchange Commission (SEC)

The SEC has direct statutory authority to prescribe accounting principles for financial statements filed with the SEC,[11] and the Securities Exchange Act of 1934 requires publicly reporting companies to keep accurate books and records and maintain adequate internal accounting controls.[12] The SEC has, for the most part, deferred to the FASB and its predecessors. However, the SEC does have its own accounting regulations and releases. **Regulation S-X**, the SEC's principal accounting regulation, prescribes accounting requirements for disclosures required by the Securities Act of 1933 and the Securities Exchange Act of 1934. The SEC also issues releases dealing with accounting issues. **Financial Reporting Releases (FRRs)**, the most important, are official statements by the SEC of accounting policies and standards. Before 1982, these releases were known as **Accounting Series Releases (ASRs)**. In 1982, the SEC incorporated all of the ASRs into Financial Reporting Release No. 1.   The SEC staff also issues its own **Staff Accounting Bulletins**, informal statements of interpretations and practices followed by the SEC staff in administering the federal securities laws.

The SEC is also an active participant in private standard-setting. The SEC's Chief Accountant is a member of the FASB Emerging Issues Task Force, and SEC commissioners and staff members often publicly state their views on accounting issues. The SEC has sometimes proposed accounting regulations that were withdrawn only after the accounting

---

[11] Securities Act of 1933 § 19(a), 15 U.S.C. § 77s(a); Securities Exchange Act of 1934 § 13(b)(1), 15 U.S.C. § 78m(b)(1).

[12] Securities Exchange Act of 1934 § 13(b)(2), 15 U.S.C. § 78m(b)(2).

profession developed its own principles. When the SEC expresses itself strongly on an issue, the private standard setters usually go along. The SEC's strong influence is undoubtedly due to the threat, implicit or explicit, that the SEC will use its statutory authority to set accounting standards on its own. On a few occasions, but not often, the SEC has overruled the private body.

Prior to the FASB

The FASB was created in 1972. Prior to that, authoritative statements on accounting principles were published by two other entities affiliated with the American Institute of Certified Public Accountants (AICPA). From 1938 to 1959, the AICPA **Committee on Accounting Procedure (CAP)** published statements on accounting principles known as **Accounting Research and Terminology Bulletins (ARBs)**. In 1959, the AICPA established the **Accounting Principles Board (APB)**. The APB, composed of 21 part-time members, published formal **Opinions** on specific accounting issues, **Interpretations** of those Opinions, and broader **Statements** designed to increase the quality of financial reporting. The APB was eliminated when the FASB was created, but the earlier opinions are still valid, unless revised or superseded by the FASB's own releases.

Even though the AICPA has ceded primary responsibility for GAAP to the FASB, it still produces audit and accounting guides and position statements through its **Accounting Standards Executive Committee (Ac-SEC)** and its **Auditing Standards Board (ASB)**. The ASB retains primary responsibility for auditing standards. The Ac-SEC's views are not enforceable standards under the AICPA Code of Professional Conduct unless the FASB adopts them, but they nevertheless provide guidance to CPAs on issues not otherwise covered by the authoritative bodies.

Other Sources of GAAP

The various publications discussed above are not the only sources of generally accepted accounting principles. In the absence of a pronouncement by one of these authorities on a particular issue, the AICPA allows accountants to rely on practices by accountants "that are widely recognized and prevalent either generally or in the industry."[13] GAAP may also be derived from other accounting literature, such as textbooks, handbooks, and articles, if no more authoritative statements are available.

---

[13] AICPA, "The Meaning of Present Fairly in Conformity With Generally Accepted Accounting Principles in the Independent Auditor's Report," SAS No. 69 (rev. June 1993).

The Internal Revenue Service

The Internal Revenue Code and the corresponding Treasury Regulations provide for accounting for federal tax purposes that is sometimes quite different from the treatment required by generally accepted accounting principles. Thus, the calculations a company does for tax purposes may differ substantially from the calculations it does to prepare its financial statements. If there is a conflict between GAAP and tax law, the requirements in the Internal Revenue Code and Treasury Regulations must be followed for tax purposes. In accounting, as in everything else, it's advisable not to cross the tax collector.

13

NOTES TO THE FINANCIAL STATEMENTS

At the bottom of almost every company's financial statements, you will find the following language, or something very similar: **"The accompanying notes are an integral part of these financial statements."** The notes referred to appear in a separate section following the financial statements with a name like *Notes to Financial Statements*. This Notes section usually covers several pages and is often quite complex.

The notes to the financial statements are very important— probably as important as the financial statements themselves—and should not be overlooked. They are not like the footnotes in law reviews, whose sole function is to put you to sleep. The notes to the financial statements are vital to understanding the numbers in the financial statements and how they were generated.

To a great extent, the notes are required, either by GAAP or by SEC rules. Both the FASB and the SEC require notes in situations where they believe the financial statements alone provide an incomplete picture. Even if a particular explanatory note is not expressly required, it may be necessary to keep the financial statements from being misleading and exposing the company to liability for fraud. A company may also voluntarily include notes because it does not feel the financial statements alone present a fair picture of the company's business or operations. The additional information in the notes allows the company to "make its case" to investors and other users of the financial statements.

Disclosure of Accounting Principles

Companies are required by GAAP to explain the accounting principles, practices, and methods they used to prepare the financial statements—how they came up with the particular numbers. This explanation usually appears at the first of the notes. The explanation of the company's accounting practices is particularly important where two or more alternative principles or approaches are acceptable under GAAP— for example, the choice among depreciation methods or different ways of valuing inventory.

Any changes in the company's accounting methods must also be reported. The financial statements usually report results for more than one period to allow a comparison of the present statements with those from prior years. The same accounting principles must usually be followed period after period, but changes from one method to another are permitted in certain circumstances. For example, a company may sometimes change the way it values inventory. A change of accounting methods from one period to the next makes it difficult to compare the results of the two periods. Any change of this sort must be disclosed in the notes. Often, the notes will restate the financial statements from the prior period using the new accounting method to make comparison easier.

Events Not Reflected in the Financial Statements

The footnotes may also contain information about events or transactions that are not reflected in the financial statements. A future contingency or commitment that is not accrued as an expense will not appear on the financial statements. The company may use the footnotes to describe the contingency. If, for example, litigation is pending against the company, the company can describe the litigation and the likelihood of success. Even if the contingency has been accrued on the financial statements, a note might still be necessary to provide additional details. The company can also use the notes to describe any significant events that occurred after the balance sheet and the income statement were prepared. For example, if the company's balance sheet shows assets and liabilities as of December 31 and the company's manufacturing plant exploded on January 2, a footnote disclosing this subsequent event can help prevent users of the balance sheet from being misled.

Other Supplemental Information

The company can also use the footnotes to provide greater detail, including non-quantitative data,[1] about items that are reported on the financial statements. It is common, for example, for companies to include a note providing additional detail about the stockholder's equity accounts: descriptions of the different classes of stock and their rights, descriptions of what produced any changes in the equity accounts, and descriptions of any outstanding stock options or rights that are not currently reflected in the equity accounts but might affect them in the future. As another example, if the company has been involved in a significant merger or acquisition, the company might explain how it accounted for the transaction and what effect the transaction had on the financial statements, so the effect of the acquisition on the financial statements can be separated from the effect of the company's regular operations.

---

[1] For those of you who still haven't mastered accounting jargon, this would be what lay people call text.

14

INTERNAL ACCOUNTING CONTROLS

Nobody—business or individual—likes to be victimized by theft or fraud, but it seems to happen often—trusted employees or agents embezzling thousands or even millions of dollars, taking bribes or kickbacks to act improperly, conspiring to produce inaccurate financial records. One of accountants' jobs is to design controls in internal accounting systems to help prevent those kinds of losses. Human nature being what it is, no accounting system can stop all fraud or theft, but good accounting controls can minimize losses.

Accounting controls are so important to businesses that entire courses are devoted to the subject.[1] You don't need that much detail. We'll briefly consider the potential problems in five areas and the controls necessary to help prevent financial loss. Most of these controls boil down to one simple lesson. A business should always keep three accounting responsibilities in separate hands: (1) the custody of assets, (2) the recording of transactions regarding those assets, and (3) the authorization to dispose of those assets. In the rest of this chapter, consider how the failure to separate these three functions can cause a loss to a business.

Cash Receipts

Cash is the favorite target of thieves for two reasons. First, it is readily converted to personal use. Unlike other property, it doesn't have to be "fenced" or sold. Second, it is fungible and difficult to trace. Unless you know the serial numbers, you can't easily tell whether the cash a person has is the same cash that was stolen.

Cash usually comes to a business when the business sells merchandise or services. A buyer may either pay in cash immediately or elect to charge the purchase and pay later. Either way, there's an opportunity for fraud.

When the buyer pays immediately, the most important control is to record the receipt of the cash. Once the receipt of the cash is recorded

---

[1] Before you criticize accountants for this, remember some of the subjects entire law school courses are devoted to.

(for example, with a cash register or the issuance of a pre-numbered sales ticket), any subsequent loss is easily detected by comparing the amount of cash on hand (e.g. in the cash drawer) to the amount that the cash register indicates *should* be on hand. If the amount of cash received is not recorded, it's difficult to determine whether any is missing, making it easier for a dishonest employee to skim the cash and hide its loss from the business.

Consider two fairly common controls used by businesses which you may have seen as a consumer. The first involves retail sales. In some stores, you will see a sign near the cash register saying something like: "If you do not receive a receipt, we will give you a $10 gift certificate. Please contact the manager to receive your gift." These signs are not to make customers happy, but to encourage employees to ring up items on the cash register.[2] Once the employee scans the item and the sale is recorded, it is easy to determine if any cash is missing from the drawer. On the other hand, if the sale is never recorded, the employee can easily pocket the cash.[3] In essence, such schemes make customers part of the company's accounting control system.

A second control is also common. When you go to a restaurant, the waitress or waiter records your order on a sales ticket. If you look closely, you'll see that the sales tickets are mechanically pre-numbered in sequence. The restaurant can easily account for all sales tickets and determine if one is missing. This prevents the employee from collecting the amount of the bill and destroying the ticket to eliminate any record of the sale.

It is also important for a business to control what happens to the cash after it's received. First, all receipts should be deposited in the firm's bank account intact. Cash needed for the business should not be taken directly from the cash receipts. Once the cash is deposited in the bank, an employee must withdraw the funds or write a check to steal it. This leaves a paper or electronic trail which makes it easier for the company to discover the theft. Cash receipts generally should be

---

[2] Some years ago, it was common for stores to have red stars print randomly on receipts. When the customer's receipt had the red star, the purchase was free. Because of the lure of possible free purchases, customers would demand the receipt.

[3] In a small family-owned grocery store one of the authors is familiar with, a cashier had nearly perfected this routine. When a customer came through the check-out line, the cashier would omit from the receipt a small item such as a $1.00 loaf of bread. When the customer began to pay, the cashier would "notice" the loaf of bread and ask if the bread was the customer's. When the customer replied that it was, the cashier would add $1.00 to the bill without entering it in the cash register. Since a customer never said, "I want the bread added to the receipt," the cashier could pocket the extra $1.00.

deposited on a daily basis. The longer the cash remains on the company premises, the greater the chance of theft.

Controls are also necessary when customers pay through the mail using checks or other instruments. A would-be thief can convert a check to personal use even if it's made out to the business. To protect against this, at least two employees should be responsible for receiving and opening the payment in the mail. When the envelope is opened, the amount of the check should be compared with the amount recorded on the enclosed bill (known as a remittance advice). One of the employees should be responsible for the check and the other employee should be responsible for the remittance advice. The amount of all the checks and the amount of all the remittance advices should be the same. If an employee converts a check to personal use, it will be immediately apparent since the two totals won't agree.

Cash Disbursements

The flip side of cash receipts is cash disbursements. If all cash receipts are deposited intact in the bank, the only easy way for an embezzler to steal money is to write a check or make an electronic withdrawal. This may seem difficult, but it's almost child's play in businesses that don't rigorously enforce a separation of duties.

Consider the case of Donald Peterson, a 57-year old high school drop-out who spent his entire "career" embezzling millions of dollars from small businesses which hired him as a bookkeeper.[4] He routinely had access to checks and he reconciled the bank statement. Few of the owners of the businesses he defrauded ever reviewed the bank statements[5] and none of the owners ever reviewed the cancelled checks. Because he had both custody of the checks and the responsibility to record and reconcile the checks, he could write checks to himself without discovery.

To prevent fraud like this, a business must insure that each disbursement is valid and that only the proper amount is paid. In a small business, this can be accomplished rather easily if the owner writes (or, at a minimum, signs) all the checks. In a larger business, all disbursements should be supported with sufficient documentation. For instance, before a retailer authorizes payment for merchandise received from a wholesaler, the retailer should have a valid copy of a purchase requisition, purchase order, receiving report, and invoice. The requisition and pur-

---

[4] "How Low-Key Style Let a Con Man Steal Millions From Bosses," WALL ST. J. (December 4, 1995).

[5] When an employer wanted to look at the bank statement, Peterson supplied a forged copy.

chase order will establish that the merchandise was really ordered, the receiving report shows that the merchandise was received in good condition, and the invoice is the bill from the supplier. If the retailer has all four of these documents, the retailer can be reasonably confident that the payment is legitimate and the amount of the invoice is correct. All four of the documents are generated outside of the department that pays, preventing the person paying the account from submitting a request for a bogus check.

Purchases

Businesses also want to be sure that only goods and services that are legitimately needed by the company are purchased and that they are purchased at the best possible price.[6] To ensure that only products which are legitimately needed are ordered, a company can require that a central inventory department (known as stores) determine when merchandise needs to be ordered. When a need is determined, stores issues a purchase requisition to the purchasing department and sends a copy to accounts payable. The purchasing department is then responsible to find the needed merchandise at the best possible price. When the supplier is determined, the purchasing department issues a purchase order to the supplier with copies to stores and the accounts payable department, and a blind copy to the receiving department.[7]

The two areas of greatest concern are (1) the purchase of material that is not needed and (2) paying too much. The first concern is addressed by having the purchasing department only order material which has been requested by stores. The second concern is harder to police. A buyer may be tempted to purchase material at a higher price (or of a lower quality) because of bribes and kickbacks from vendors. The subjective nature of quality judgments makes it hard to tell when the buyer is paying too much or buying an inferior product.

Payroll

Payroll is another area providing an opportunity for fraud. The objectives here are to ensure that only valid employees receive a check, that the checks are for the correct amount, and that the company complies with all governmental regulations.

---

[6] "Best" does not necessarily mean "lowest." The lowest price may not be the best after considering factors such as quality and the reliability of the vendor.

[7] A blind purchase order is one which does not indicate the quantity ordered. This forces the receiving department to count the merchandise received and not just assume that the correct amount was sent. Interestingly, it is common for suppliers to include a packing slip with the merchandise which indicates the quantity shipped. This may eliminate the benefits of the blind purchase order.

It's easy to accomplish these goals when the organization separates (1) hiring and the determination of pay rates (authorization), (2) the calculation and preparation of the actual paychecks and accompanying tax information (recording), and (3) the distribution of the checks (custody). The authorization function is generally delegated to the personnel department; the preparation of the checks takes place in the payroll department; and the distribution of the checks is done by an independent paymaster.

Consider the possible problems when a company does not separate these functions. Assume that ABC, Inc. allows its production supervisor to hire employees directly. When the supervisor hires an employee, she sends the new employee's name, social security number, and other information to the payroll department. Each week, the supervisor submits approved time cards for her employees to the payroll department. Payroll prepares the checks and sends them to the supervisor to distribute.

Nothing in this system prevents the supervisor from creating a ghost employee and keeping the paycheck when it is given to her to distribute. Or the supervisor may continue to submit a time card for an employee who quits or is fired. If the checks were distributed by an independent paymaster, the supervisor could not do this.[8]

Conclusion

As you can see, the key to effective internal accounting controls is the separation of different functions. This separation makes it very difficult for a single person to defraud the company. But even the strictest separation of functions can't protect against collusion. If different employees get together to cheat the company, the prevention and detection of fraud become more difficult. As we said earlier, no system is foolproof.

In addition, the benefits of accounting controls must be balanced against their costs. A company may be willing to tolerate some losses if the cost of accounting controls to prevent the losses would be greater than the loss prevented. If this is the case, the company would be better off financially just tolerating the losses. For example, a grocery store

---

[8] A stunning example of the need to separate these functions involves the Los Angeles Dodgers. The Dodgers had such complete faith in their payroll chief, Edward Campos, that they allowed him to authorize payroll, record the payments, and have custody of the paychecks. This monumental control deficiency allowed Campos to embezzle several hundred thousand dollars. His embezzlement was easily discovered in 1986 when Campos became ill and someone else had to perform his duties. The replacement discovered that some employees earning $7 per hour were receiving paychecks of nearly $2,000 each week. Paul Feldman, "7 Accused of Embezzling $332,583 From Dodgers," L.A. TIMES, Sept. 16, 1986.

concerned about shoplifting losses could position armed guards at each aisle and shoot to kill any customer suspected of shoplifting. This would probably eliminate most of the shoplifting, but the costs of such a policy, both the cost of paying the guards and the cost in customer relations, would be greater than the benefits.

15

AUDITING

Most publicly-owned companies and some other companies have their financial statements **audited**. An **auditor** is an accountant who examines the company's accounting system to determine the reliability of the company's financial statements. A company may have its own **internal auditors**, company employees who monitor the company's accounting controls and report problems to management. But the more important audit for publicly-owned companies is the independent audit conducted by certified public accountants (CPAs). CPAs are not employees of the company; they are independent outside accountants hired to examine the company's accounting statements and opine on their accuracy. They issue **audit opinions** that indicate whether the company's financial statements were prepared in accordance with generally accepted accounting principles (GAAP). These audit opinions appear with the company's financial statements and are relied on by outsiders such as lenders and investors.

If the auditor finds a material problem with the financial statements, the opinion will be **qualified**: it will indicate that the auditor does not believe the statements are consistent with GAAP and will explain why. If the auditor finds no material problem, she will issue a **clean**, or **unqualified**, opinion.

The typical clean audit opinion has three parts. The first part explains that the financial statements are the responsibility of the company's management and that the auditor is not a guarantor of the financial statements' accuracy. The main purpose of this part of the opinion is to cover a certain portion of the auditor's posterior anatomy and help protect the auditor from lawsuits if there's a problem after the audit.

The second part of the audit opinion explains the scope of the auditor's work—which financial statements the auditor reviewed and how he conducted his work. Rather than go into great detail, this section of the opinion will usually just state that the auditor conducted his investigation in accordance with **generally accepted auditing standards (GAAS)**. GAAS are auditors' equivalent of GAAP—standards pursuant to which audits are supposed to be conducted.

The third part of the audit opinion states the auditor's opinion. If all is well, this part says that the financial statements are in conformity with generally accepted accounting principles.

A clean audit opinion will look like the following example:

> We have audited the accompanying balance sheet of X Corporation as of December 31, 1995 and 1996, and the related statements of income, retained earnings, and cash flows for the years then ended. These financial statements are the responsibility of the Company's management. Our responsibility is to express an opinion on these financial statements based on our audits.
>
> We conducted our audits in accordance with generally accepted auditing standards. These standards require that we plan and perform the audit to obtain reasonable assurance about whether the financial statements are free of material misstatement. An audit includes examining, on a test basis, evidence supporting the amounts and disclosures in the financial statements. An audit also includes assessing the accounting principles used and significant estimates made by management, as well as evaluating the overall financial statement presentation. We believe that our audits provide a reasonable basis for our opinion.
>
> In our opinion, the financial statements referred to above present fairly, in all material respects, the financial position of X Corporation as of December 31, 1994 and 1995, and the results of its operations and its cash flows for the years then ended in conformity with generally accepted accounting principles.
>
> /s/ Dense & Obtuse
> Certified Public Accountants
> January 30, 1997

This opinion is the auditor's version of the clean bill of health. Applying generally accepted auditing standards, the auditor found nothing materially wrong. If you see exceptions or qualifications—anything other than this basic language, you need to pay careful attention to the opinion.

SECTION FIVE:

THE UNCERTAINTY OF ACCOUNTING

16

THE UNCERTAINTY OF ACCOUNTING

Introduction

Accounting produces numbers, and numbers provide a reassuring sense of certainty and security. Many law students believe that numbers aren't as malleable as the words they encounter in their casebooks, which some professors seem to be able to reshape to mean whatever they want. Six dollars is six dollars, they believe, and no amount of deconstruction is going to make it otherwise. But the numbers in financial statements aren't really that certain. Accounting, like the law, is subject to judgment, interpretation, and manipulation.

Mathematics is certain.[1] Problems of addition and subtraction require no judgment. Two plus two in base 10 is always four, absolutely, without exception. Natural science is certain.[2] When you drop a rock, it falls to the ground. No amount of lobbying by special interest groups, whining about how gravity disproportionately benefits one group, or even relocation of the rock to a foreign country can change the law of gravity.

Accounting rules, on the other hand, are man-made; they vary from time to time and place to place. They can be changed if enough people don't like the results they produce. They require judgment and are subject to exceptions. Two plus two can be four, or three, or five, depending on how you treat it. Like the words in your casebooks, the numbers in accounting statements require interpretation. You can't completely accept them at face value; you have to poke around a little to see what they mean.

In this chapter, we'll give you some examples of the uncertainty of accounting and how accounting numbers can be legitimately manipulated. In the space available, we can't make you an expert on accounting manipulations. We merely hope to disabuse you of any remaining notions about the certainty and reliability of accounting and get you to treat financial statements with the same caution you'd give legal opinions.

---

[1] Mathematicians might disagree, but who pays any attention to mathematicians?
[2] If you're a natural scientist, you might disagree. Go tell a mathematician.

Depreciation, Depletion, and Amortization

In Chapter 8, we discussed depreciation, depletion, and amortization. When a company purchases an asset it expects to last for several years, the cost of that asset must be allocated as an expense over its useful life. That allocation is called depreciation, depletion, or amortization, depending on what kind of asset is involved.[3]

Depreciation introduces several uncertainties into accounting. First, you must estimate[4] the asset's useful life—the period over which its cost will be spread. When you buy a computer for $2,000, what is its expected useful life? Four years? Five years? Six years? Your estimate must be reasonably based on economic circumstances; you can't just choose a figure with no basis in reality, such as 400 years. But estimating useful life requires judgment and reasonable people can differ. Second, you must estimate the asset's salvage value. When you're finished with the computer, how much could you get rid of it for? Two hundred dollars? Four hundred dollars? Six hundred dollars? Again, this is a judgment call, and the value chosen will affect the amount of depreciation expense.

Assume that you're using the straight-line method of depreciation, allocating the depreciable cost of the computer equally over its useful life. The annual depreciation expense is the computer's cost minus its salvage value, divided by the number of years of useful life. If you think the computer's useful life is four years, with a salvage value of $200, your annual depreciation expense will be $450—$2,000 minus $200, divided by 4. If you estimate a useful life of six years and a salvage value of $500, your annual depreciation expense will be only $250. It's the same computer, but the expense (and therefore net income) is different because your estimate is different.

Estimating an asset's useful life and salvage value make depreciation uncertain, but the greatest opportunity for manipulation comes in the choice of depreciation method. As we explained in Chapter 8, you can depreciate assets in several different ways—the straight-line method, the unit-of-output method, the double-declining-balance method, and the sum-of-the-years'-digits method. Even if you are absolutely certain about the asset's useful life and salvage value, the depreciation expense from period to period will still vary depending on the method you choose.

Inventory

In Chapter 9, we discussed inventory and the Cost of Goods Sold. When goods are sold, the cost of those goods is an expense. But if your

---

[3] To simplify the discussion, we'll use the term "depreciation" to include all three.
[4] "Estimate" is a distinguished word for "guess." Non-accountants guess; accountants estimate.

THE UNCERTAINTY OF ACCOUNTING   93

inventory consists of a number of units purchased at different times for different prices, how do you determine the cost of the ones you sold? As we indicated in Chapter 9, several different methods are available—the FIFO (first-in, first-out) method, the LIFO (last-in, first-out) method, and the average cost method. Each method can produce a different Cost of Goods Sold expense, a different net income, and a different balance sheet value for the remaining inventory.

Contingencies

In Chapter 10, we discussed how to account for contingencies: events that may or may not happen at some time in the future. We told you that contingent gains are almost never recognized until they actually occur, but contingent losses sometimes must be recognized before they occur. If a contingent loss (such as losing a lawsuit or not collecting an account receivable) is probable to occur in the future, and the amount of the loss can be reasonably estimated, that estimated amount must be treated as a current expense.The uncertainty this test introduces is obvious. First, the company, its accountants, and its attorneys must decide whether the contingency is probable: Are we likely to lose this lawsuit? Will we probably be unable to collect this account receivable? This prediction of the future requires judgment, and reasonable people can differ.⁵ Second, if the contingency is probable, what's a reasonable estimate of the amount of the loss? Will we have to pay $45,000 damages if we lose the lawsuit, or $50,000, or $55,000? Again, reasonable people can estimate differently.

One company might not recognize a contingent loss at all, concluding that it's not probable to occur. Another company might decide that the identical contingency is probable to occur, and recognize a loss of $50,000, its reasonable estimate of the amount. A third company might agree that the contingency is probable, but conclude that a reasonable estimate of the amount is $40,000. The contingency is the same for all three companies, but their financial statements will be quite different.

Shifting Income Among Related Companies

Another way to manipulate financial statements is to shift income among related companies.

To understand how this works, assume that you own 100 percent of two different companies—a professional baseball team and a television station. The television station is negotiating a contract to broadcast the baseball team's games. If the contract payment is large, the team is

---

⁵ Even accountants, who aren't reasonable people, can differ.

more profitable and the station is less profitable. If the contract payment is small, the team is less profitable and the station is more profitable. Either way, however, your total profits are the same, because you own both companies.

But what if the team has to pay the players a share of its profits? You have an incentive to make the team's profits appear smaller. To accomplish this, you could have your television station pay the team only a small amount for the broadcast rights. This minimizes the team's profits (which you have to share with the players) and maximizes the station's profits (which you don't have to share).

If, on the other hand, you are interested in selling the team, you might want to make the team's income appear greater. In that case, you could increase the television station's payment, maximizing the team's profits and minimizing the station's profits.

Because you own both companies, you can shift the income from broadcasting the games to whichever company you want. The economic effect on you is the same, but the financial statements are different.

Consider another example. CarCo manufactures an automobile known as the Venus, which sells for $15,000 retail. GoFast Engines, Inc. makes the engines for the Venus and sells them to CarCo for $9,000 each. The car's other parts cost $3,500, the cost to assemble the car is $1,500, and CarCo pays a $1,000 sales commission for each car sold. If you add up these expenses, they total $15,000, which is the price at which CarCo is selling the car. CarCo has no net income, and it seems senseless for it to continue to produce the cars.

But let's take a closer look. It costs GoFast $3,000 to produce each engine and ship it to CarCo, so GoFast makes a profit of $6,000 on each car. CarCo owns 100 percent of GoFast, so profits to GoFast are in effect profits to CarCo. Why set the engine price so high that all the profit goes to GoFast instead of CarCo? CarCo is a U.S. company and has to pay U.S. income taxes on its income. GoFast makes the engines in a foreign country in which companies pay no income taxes. By setting the price so high that GoFast receives all of the profit on the cars, CarCo is able to avoid a major expense, income tax payments.[6] The two related companies are able to manipulate their financial statements to their benefit.

One way to avoid some of the manipulation between related companies is to require what are known as **consolidated financial statements**. A consolidated financial statement presents a financial picture of all the related companies together, as if they were a single company. In the example above, CarCo and GoFast would have a single, combined balance sheet and a single, combined income statement. The financial

---

[6] It isn't this easy in real life, but the idea is the same.

statements of large, publicly-held companies are often presented on a consolidated basis. If the financial statements are consolidated, income-shifting is less important because the combined income statement and balance sheet will look the same no matter how the income is allocated.

Mergers and Acquisitions

Another area where manipulation is possible requires accounting expertise beyond the scope of this book, but is worth mentioning. Two separate companies sometimes combine to create a single company. This can be done in many ways: (1) by one company purchasing all the assets of the other, (2) by a statutory device known as a merger, (3) by having the shareholders of one or both of the companies exchange stock, or (4) by a purchase of stock known as a tender offer. The details of those various devices are beyond the scope of this book. All you need to know is that companies can manipulate their financial statements by varying the structure of the deal. Transactions whose end result and economic effect are practically identical can be accounted for in very different ways. It would take dozens of pages to give you the details, and even some accountants have trouble with the rules.[7] Just be warned that if you're looking at a company that was involved in a combination like this, you need to review the accounting details pretty carefully to see how the transaction affected the company's financial statements.

Historical Cost Versus Market Value

Finally, remember that accounting statement values are based on historical cost—what you paid for assets. An asset's value on the financial statements may not be its market value. For example, immediately after World War II, you could have purchased land in downtown Tokyo very cheaply. Let's assume you bought ten lots for $100,000. Today, those ten lots would be worth millions of dollars, but your balance sheet would still show their original purchase price, $100,000. If you sold the land and actually realized the profit, the gain would show up on your financial statements. Until then, the accounting principle of conservatism forces you to list the land at its historical cost.

When you're looking at financial statements, particularly the balance sheet, you should keep this in mind. The numbers you're looking at are

---

[7] If you really insist on being confused, the applicable accounting rules are in two Accounting Principles Board opinions. *See* Accounting Principles Board, Opinion No. 16 (1970); Accounting Principles Board, Opinion No. 18 (1971). For an explanation of these rules, *see* Robert S. Kay & D. Gerald Searfoss, HANDBOOK OF ACCOUNTING AND AUDITING chap. 23 (2d ed. 1989).

history and may not tell you a lot about the current market values—the true economic worth—of the company's assets and liabilities.

An Example of Accounting Uncertainty

The best way to appreciate the uncertainty of accounting is to see it in action. Let's take two identical companies, run them through equivalent transactions, and see how we can use the rules of accounting to make them appear different. And we'll keep the transactions relatively simple to prove that accounting numbers can be manipulated even for uncomplicated transactions.

We'll call our two companies Alpha Company and Beta Company. They have identical assets and no liabilities. Their balance sheets at the end of 1995 are identical, as follows:

Alpha and Beta Companies			
Balance Sheets			
As of December 31, 1995			
Assets		*Liabilities and Equity*	
Cash	$1,500,000	Liabilities	$ 0
Widgets	700,000	Equity	2,300,000
Land	100,000	Total Liabilities	
Total Assets	$2,300,000	and Equity	$2,300,000

This is our starting point, and it's obviously a very simple one. Now let's look at what happens to these companies in 1996 and see how different we can make them look.

Transaction 1—Purchase of a Computer System. In 1996, Alpha and Beta purchased identical computer systems for $50,000 cash.

Alpha estimated that the system has a useful life of 10 years and a salvage value of $5,000. The depreciable cost is $50,000 - $5,000 = $45,000. Using the straight-line method of depreciation, Alpha's depreciation expense for the year is $4,500, $1/10$ of the system's depreciable cost. The net book value of the system on Alpha's balance sheet, after subtracting the accumulated depreciation, is $45,500.

Beta estimated that the system has a useful life of 8 years and a salvage value of $2,000. Beta uses the double-declining-balance method of calculating depreciation. Its depreciation expense for the year is $12,500 and the net book value of the system on Beta's balance sheet, after subtracting accumulated depreciation, is $37,500.

Transaction 2—Changes to Inventory. At the beginning of 1996, each company owned 2,000 widgets, purchased a couple of years ago for $350 each (resulting in the Widgets value of $700,000 on the December 31, 1995 balance sheets). In 1996, each company purchased 1,000 more widgets for $500 a widget, and sold 1,000 widgets for $700 a widget.

The sales revenue for both companies is $700,000 ($700 x 1,000 widgets). Alpha determines its Cost of Goods Sold using the FIFO method of inventory valuation. Its Cost of Goods Sold (an expense) is $350,000 ($350 x 1,000 widgets). Its ending inventory (the book value of the Widgets on the balance sheet) will be $850,000—the beginning inventory, $700,000, plus the purchases, $500,000, minus the Cost of Goods Sold, $350,000.

Beta determines its Cost of Goods Sold using the LIFO method of inventory valuation. Its Cost of Goods Sold is $500,000 ($500 x 1000 widgets). Its ending inventory (the book value of the Widgets) will be $700,000—the beginning inventory, $700,000, plus the purchases, $500,000, minus the Cost of Goods Sold, $500,000.

Transaction 3: Collectibility of Accounts Receivable. The 1,000 widgets each company sold were sold on credit, rather than for cash, creating Accounts Receivable of $700,000. The buyers were identical for both companies.

Alpha estimates that 2% of these accounts receivable will not be collected. Its Uncollectible Accounts Expense is 2 percent of the total, $14,000. On the balance sheet, the book value of its Accounts Receivable will be offset by a $14,000 Allowance for Uncollectible Accounts.

Beta estimates that 5% of these accounts receivable will not be collected. Its Uncollectible Accounts Expense is 5 percent of the total, $35,000, and the book value of its Accounts Receivable will be offset by a $35,000 Allowance for Uncollectible Accounts.

Transaction 4: Land. At the beginning of 1996, each company owned undeveloped real estate in Los Angeles, purchased in 1914 for $100,000. This land is listed on the December 31, 1995 balance sheets at its historical cost.

In January, Alpha sold its land for $10 million cash. This sale increased Alpha's cash by $10 million, eliminated the $100,000 in the Land account, and produced a profit of $9,900,000 (the $10 million sales price minus the cost of the land). In December, Alpha decided its original decision was wrong and it purchased an identical piece of property for $10 million. The subsequent purchase created a new Land account with a book value of $10 million and reduced Alpha's cash by $10 million. The net result of the two transactions is no change to the Cash account, a $9,900,000 profit, and an increase in the Land account from $100,000 to $10 million.

Beta kept its land throughout 1996, so its financial statements didn't change. Note that, although Alpha's and Beta's actions differ, the two companies are still in an identical position at the end of the year. Each owns an identical parcel of land and each has the same amount of cash.

The Result of these Transactions. Alpha and Beta began and finished the year in identical positions, but look at what happened to their financial statements. First, let's examine their respective income statements for 1996, set forth below:

Alpha Company
Income Statement
For Calendar Year 1996

Revenues:

Sales of Widgets	$ 700,000	
Sale of Land	10,000,000	
Total Revenues		$10,700,000

Expenses:

Depreciation	$ 4,500	
Cost of Goods Sold	350,000	
Uncollectible Accounts	14,000	
Cost of Land Sold	100,000	
Total Expenses		468,500
Net Income		$10,231,500

Beta Company
Income Statement
For Calendar Year 1996

Revenues:

Sales of Widgets	$ 700,000	
Total Revenues		$ 700,000

Expenses:

Depreciation	$ 12,500	
Cost of Goods Sold	500,000	
Uncollectible Accounts	35,000	
Total Expenses		547,500
Net Income		$152,500

Note the differences. Alpha's income statement shows $10 million revenue from the sale of land and a corresponding expense of $100,000.

Beta had no such sale, so nothing comparable appears on Beta's income statement. The depreciation expenses differ because of different estimates of useful life and salvage value and because the companies use different methods of depreciation. The costs of goods sold differ because the companies use different methods of valuing inventory, and the uncollectible accounts expenses differ because of different estimates of collectibility. The net result is that Alpha has a net income of $10,231,500 and Beta has a net income of only $152,500. The companies' real financial positions are still identical at the end of the year, but the accounting statements look very different.

Now, compare the two companies' balance sheets as of the end of 1996. Again, the differences are dramatic:

Alpha Company
Balance Sheet
As of December 31, 1996

Assets			*Liabilities and Equity*		
Cash		$ 950,000			
Widgets		850,000	Liabilities	$	0
Land		10,000,000	Equity		12,531,500
Computer	$50,000				
Less:Accum. Deprec.	4,500	45,500			
Accts. Receiv.	$700,000				
Less: Allowance for					
Uncollectible Accts.	14,000	$ 686,000	Total Liabilities		
Total Assets		$12,531,500	and Equity		$12,531,500

Beta Company
Balance Sheet
As of December 31, 1996

Assets			*Liabilities and Equity*		
Cash		$ 950,000			
Widgets		700,000	Liabilities	$	0
Land		100,000	Equity		2,452,500
Computer	$50,000				
Less:Accum. Deprec.	12,500	37,500			
Accts. Receiv.	$700,000				
Less: Allowance for					
Uncollectible Accts.	35,000	$ 665,000	Total Liabilities		
Total Assets		$2,452,500	and Equity		$2,452,500

The net book value of Alpha's assets at the end of 1996 is $12,531,500, compared to $2,452,500 for Beta. The reasons for this difference? Their different inventory valuation methods produce different values for the widgets, even though they both have identical sets of widgets. Alpha's sale and repurchase of land produces a different book value for the land, even though the two properties are identical. The different approaches to depreciation affect the book value of the computer systems, and the different estimates of collectibility affect the book value of the accounts receivable. The two companies are identical in all respects, but their accounting statements are dramatically different.

We've been able to produce these differences using very simple balance sheets and only a few straightforward transactions. No sophisticated financial sleight-of-hand was involved. If we can produce differences like this using such simple transactions, imagine what huge multi-million dollar conglomerates can do with more sophisticated transactions and accounting techniques. Always remember: accounting is neither certain nor free of manipulation, even if accountants strictly follow generally accepted accounting principles (GAAP). You always need to look behind the numbers.

SECTION SIX:

OTHER VALUATION CONCEPTS

17

COST ACCOUNTING

Cost Accounting

How much does it cost? This question, which parents have been asking for generations,[1] also concerns accountants. **Cost accounting** deals with the collection and interpretation of information about costs. The purpose of cost accounting is to determine the cost of particular products or operations. How much does it cost to produce a can of beans?[2] Which costs more—boxing cans of beans by hand or using an automatic boxing machine?

Cost accounting is extremely important to the managers of businesses. They want to minimize costs and maximize profits and they can't do that without reliable cost data. The idea of cost is also important to economists. Many economic analyses, including economic analyses of law, turn on notions of cost.

The determination and allocation of costs is a difficult accounting problem requiring a sophisticated knowledge of accounting. We won't discuss the details of cost accounting, only some of the basic principles lawyers and law students should know.

Fixed Costs, Variable Costs, and Total Cost

Costs—whether they be the costs of manufacturing a product, the costs of driving a car, or the costs of attending law school—can be split into two categories: **fixed costs** and **variable costs**. A **fixed cost** is one that remains unchanged despite changes in volume. "Volume" in this definition means the amount of the activity in question—such as the number of units of a product manufactured, the number of miles a car is driven, or the number of credit-hours of law school attended. Assume, for example, that you must buy a law dictionary to attend law school.

---

[1] As in the following dialogue:

Child: "I gotta have the new Slappo 1500Z Atomic, Laser-Guided, Modulated Destructo Alien-Blaster."

Parent: "How much does it cost?"

Child: "Only $97,000."

[2] Insert your own bean-counter joke here.

The cost of the dictionary is a fixed cost of attending law school. Whether you take 3, 6, 9, 12, or any other number of credit-hours, you need only one dictionary. The cost of the dictionary is fixed. It does not vary with the number of credit-hours you take.

A *variable cost* is one that increases and decreases as volume increases and decreases. The cost of the paper you use to take notes in class is a variable cost of attending law school. It varies with the number of credit-hours you take. The more credit-hours you take, the more notes you'll take, and the more paper you'll need.[3]

The distinction between fixed and variable costs is not as definite as you might think. Most costs categorized as fixed costs are not really fixed for all possible volumes. Consider, for example, the cost of building a factory to manufacture bicycles. The cost of building the factory is a fixed cost of manufacturing bicycles. It is the same whether the factory produces one, two, three, or a thousand bicycles. At some point, however, the factory will be producing at full capacity. If the company wants to make more bicycles than that, it must build a new factory or expand the old one. The cost of the factory, like most fixed costs, is not really fixed for all possible amounts of production. Because of this problem, a fixed cost is better defined as a cost that does not change within some relevant range of volume.

The *total cost* of any activity is the sum of all the fixed and variable costs. Thus, the total cost of attending law school for three years is the sum of all the costs you pay, whether fixed or variable, that are attributable to your law school attendance: the cost of tuition, books, antacid, and so on. The concept of total cost is more difficult than it sounds; most of the complexity of cost accounting arises in trying to decide which costs are appropriately charged to which activity. For example, when you go out to lunch with a classmate to discuss your Evidence class, is the cost of the lunch a cost of attending law school? You would have had to eat even if you weren't attending law school, so the cost of eating isn't really a cost of law school. But what if you usually eat a brown-bag lunch and you went out to eat only because your classmate refused to discuss Evidence anywhere else? Or consider a corporate executive who is responsible for several different products. If the company wants to determine the total cost of producing each product, how much of the executive's salary should it allocate to each? These examples

---

[3] Sometimes, accountants reserve the term *variable cost* to mean only costs that increase or decrease in direct proportion to changes in volume: when volume increases 10 percent, the variable cost increases 10 percent. They call a cost that varies, but not in direct proportion to volume, a *semivariable* or *mixed cost*. However, economists (and most lawyers) usually use the term variable cost to refer to any cost that changes as volume changes, whether or not the change is proportionate.

give you just a glimpse of the difficulties of cost accounting; this chapter only scratches the surface.

Measuring Cost Per Unit: Average Total Cost and Marginal Cost

Total cost measures the total cost of any given volume—the total cost of driving your car 10,000 miles, the total cost of manufacturing 100,000 bicycles, the total cost of attending law school for three years. Two other cost concepts measure the cost per unit of volume—the cost of driving your car one mile, the cost to produce a single bicycle, the cost of one credit-hour of law school.

One measure of cost per unit, **average total cost**, is simply the total cost of producing all units divided by the total number of units produced. If the total cost of driving your car 10,000 miles is $1,000, the average total cost is 10 cents per mile. If the total cost to produce 10 bicycles is $1,500, the average total cost is $150 per bicycle. If the total cost of 90 credit-hours of law school is $90 billion, the average total cost is $1 billion per credit-hour.

Total cost, you will recall, is the sum of all fixed costs and all variable costs. Occasionally, average total cost is split into these two component elements. **Average fixed cost** is the sum of all fixed costs divided by the number of units. **Average variable cost** is the sum of all variable costs divided by the number of units. Since fixed costs plus variable costs equal total cost, the sum of the average fixed cost and the average variable cost must equal the average total cost.

Another measure of the cost of a unit is **marginal cost**. Average total cost measures the average cost of producing all of the units; marginal cost measures the cost of producing one particular unit. Marginal cost is the additional cost of producing a particular unit after the units that came before it have been produced. The marginal cost of driving the 10,000th mile in your car is the additional cost of going one more mile after you've already driven 9,999—the cost of the small additional amount of gas and the slight additional wear on the car. The marginal cost of taking Corporations in law school consists of the extra costs you incur just for Corporations—the casebook, some extra paper for notes, the extraordinary boredom.[4] The marginal cost of producing the tenth bicycle is the additional cost incurred to produce the tenth bicycle after the company has already produced the first nine. If it costs $1,400 to produce nine bicycles and $1,500 to produce ten, the marginal cost of producing the tenth one is $100. Note that this differs from the average

---

[4] The law professor author of this book teaches Corporations. He assumes that his students' boredom stems from the subject, not the teacher. The law professor's wife isn't so sure.

total cost of producing the ten bicycles, which is $150 per bicycle ($1,500 ÷ 10). Marginal cost and average total cost often differ.

An Example: The Cost of Operating a Law School

To help you understand these concepts, let's consider the cost of operating a new law school. Before a law school admits its first student, it must have a building with classrooms and office space, it must hire faculty to teach the courses, and it must hire administrators to run the school.[5] Assume that the school hires 10 faculty members and two administrators and builds a new building. All of this costs $2 million. The school must also prepare records for each student, which we'll assume costs $5 per student. You need other things, like a good psychiatrist, to run a law school, but, to keep it simple, assume that these are the only costs.

The total cost to educate one law student is $2,000,005—the cost of the building, faculty, and administrators, plus the record keeping cost for that student. This is also the marginal cost of educating the first law student—the additional cost incurred to educate one law student instead of none. Total cost and marginal cost are identical when only one unit of output is produced, because all of the fixed costs are part of the marginal cost for the first unit.

If the school admits a second student, it doesn't have to build another building or hire additional faculty and administrators. The existing building, faculty, and staff can easily accommodate both students. These costs are fixed costs; they don't vary with the number of students. The only additional cost associated with the second student is a slight increase in record keeping; the school must now prepare and maintain records on the second student, at an additional cost of $5. The record keeping cost is a variable cost; it varies with the number of students. The total cost of educating two law students is $2,000,010. The average total cost of educating these two law students is $1,000,005—the total cost, $2,000,010, divided by the number of students, 2. However, the marginal cost of educating the second law student is only $5. The only additional cost of adding the second student is the cost of the additional record keeping.

If the school adds a third student, it still doesn't need a new building or more faculty or administrators. The only additional cost is the additional record keeping cost, $5. Thus, the marginal cost of educating the

---

[5] The law professor author of this book believes that faculty members are the most important component of a law school. The accountant author believes that the most important component of a law school must be the administrators, to keep people like the law professor author in line.

third student is only $5. The total cost of educating all three law students is $2,000,015. The average total cost of educating these three law students is approximately $666,672—the total cost $2,000,015, divided by the total number of students, 3.

The same trend continues as the size of the class increases to 4, 5, 6, and more students. The costs of the building, the faculty, and the administrators do not increase; over this range, those costs are fixed. The only additional cost, a variable cost, is the cost of the extra paperwork for each student. The marginal cost of each additional student remains $5, so the total cost increases by $5 for each additional student, and the average total cost decreases as we divide the large fixed costs by more and more students.

At some point, however, the number of students will get so large that more faculty and administrators, and perhaps also more classroom space, will be needed. These costs, which are fixed over some range of students, increase after enrollment reaches a certain number. As we stated earlier, "fixed" costs are usually fixed only over a certain range of output. Once you exceed that output, the "fixed" costs increase.

18

PRESENT VALUE
AND THE TIME VALUE OF MONEY

The next two chapters deal with principles of valuation used more by financial analysts than by accountants. Although they aren't technically accounting principles, they are still very important for lawyers and law students to know. In this chapter, we explore *present value*, *future value*, and the *time value of money*. In the next chapter, we discuss another important valuation concept, *expected value*.

The Time Value of Money

A dollar received now is worth more than a dollar to be received sometime in the future. A dollar paid now costs more than a dollar to be paid sometime in the future. This critical idea is known as the *time value of money*.

Assume that we offer to give you $100.[1] We give you a choice: you can have one hundred U.S. dollars or one hundred Canadian dollars. Since you're reasonably intelligent,[2] you know that U.S. and Canadian dollars aren't equivalent just because they're both called "dollars." The U.S. dollar is more valuable; it has greater purchasing power. You'll choose one hundred U.S. dollars, because they're worth more than one hundred Canadian dollars.

We now give you a second choice: you can take the $100 now or you can wait and receive it in one year. You should take the $100 now, but why?

One answer is that you may not trust us. One of us is, after all, a law professor. You may fear that, a year from now, we will change our minds and not pay you or, more likely, we'll be broke and unable to pay you. If you take the money now, you don't risk nonpayment. In the next chapter, we'll discuss the effect uncertainty and risk have on value. But, even if you were absolutely sure you'd get the money in a year, $100

---

[1] Ignore the obvious flaws in this hypothetical: No accounting or law professor would have $100 cash to give away and, even if we had it, the likelihood that we'd give it to a student is infinitesimally small.

[2] After all, you're a law student, not an accounting student.

now is still more valuable. Like the Canadian dollars and the U.S. dollars, the $100 now and the $100 in one year are not equivalent. A dollar today is not the same as a dollar in the future.

If you take the money now, you can spend it immediately or, if you don't need it now, you can invest it and have more than $100 in a year. Assume that, if you take the $100 now and don't spend it, you can invest it and earn 6% annual interest. The $100 we give you today would grow to $106 after a year, the original $100 plus the interest.[3] The **_future value_** in one year of $100 today is $106. To put it another way, if the annual interest rate is 6 percent, having $100 now is equivalent to having $106 in one year. Since $100 now is equivalent to $106 in one year, you clearly prefer $100 now to $100 in one year.

If the choice is between $100 now and $100 _two_ years from now, the difference is even greater. If you take $100 now and invest it at 6 percent interest, you would have $106 after one year. If you reinvest the $106 and earn the same 6 percent interest for the second year, you would have $112.36 by the end of the second year. This is clearly better than receiving $100 two years from now.[4] Notice that you earn $6.00 interest in the first year, and $6.36 interest in the second year. In the second year, you're earning 6% interest not only on the original $100, but also on the $6 interest you earned in the first year. The extra 36 cents is the interest on your first year's interest (6 percent of $6.00). This interest on interest is known as **_compound interest_**.

The future value of any amount of money is simply the amount plus the interest you could earn on it. The future value one year from now of $1 today is

$$\text{FV (1 year)} = \$1 \times (1 + r),$$

where r is the annual rate of interest expressed in decimal form (for example, 4 percent equals .04).[5] Thus, if the rate of interest is 10%, the future value of $1 in one year is

$$
\begin{aligned}
\text{FV} &= \$1 \times (1 + .10) \\
&= \$1 \times 1.10 \\
&= \$1.10
\end{aligned}
$$

---

[3] This assumes that you don't have to pay taxes on your interest income. If you have to pay taxes, your after-tax interest, at current tax rates, would be approximately three cents.

[4] The accountant author would like to note that even the lawyer author can understand that $112 is better than $100. The lawyer author believes the accountant author is overcompensating for the inherent inferiority of accountants.

[5] We believe that "i" would make more sense than "r", but these formulas were developed by quantitative types who weren't particularly logical.

More generally, the future value in one year of any amount "A" is

$$FV \text{ (1 year)} = A \times (1 + r).$$

Applying the formula, if the rate of interest is 5%, the value in one year of $150 is

$$
\begin{aligned}
FV &= \$150 \times (1 + .05) \\
&= \$150 \times 1.05 \\
&= \$157.50
\end{aligned}
$$

The future value in two years of any amount "A" is simply the value after the first year multiplied by the interest rate again:

$$FV \text{ (2 years)} = A \times (1 + r) \times (1 + r).$$

The future value in three years of that same amount would just be the value after the second year multiplied by the interest rate again:

$$FV \text{ (3 years)} = A \times (1 + r) \times (1 + r) \times (1 + r)$$

To determine how much any given amount will be worth n years from now, you simply multiply by the interest factor, $(1 + r)$, n times. Using exponential notation, the formula to determine the future value of "A" dollars at the end of n years is:

$$FV \text{ (n years)} = A \times (1 + r)^n.$$

For those of you unfamiliar with exponential notation, the superscript "n" in the formula is simply another way of indicating that you should multiply by $(1 + r)$ n times. Thus, the future value of $50 after 5 years, if the rate of interest is 6 percent, is:

$$
\begin{aligned}
FV &= \$50 \times (1 + .06)^5 \\
&= \$50 \times (1.06) \times (1.06) \times (1.06) \times (1.06) \times (1.06) \\
&= \$66.91
\end{aligned}
$$

We don't recommend that you solve equations like this using pencil and paper. You can do this easily on a calculator. In fact, many calculators have present value and future value keys that allow you to input the amount, the number of years, and the interest rate, and the calculator does all the work for you. You don't even have to know the formula.

Present Value

Present value is just the opposite of future value. Future value measures the value in the future of a payment now; present value measures the value now of a payment to be made in the future. The interest rate used to calculate present value is called the **discount rate**. The discount rate measures how much the delay in receiving money costs a person. The discount rate is essentially the return the person could have earned on the money in the time prior to payment.

To understand present value, you need only reverse the future value calculations we just did. If $100 today is worth $106 in one year, then the present value of $106 to be paid in one year is $100. Present value is the amount that, if you had it now, you could invest and produce an amount equivalent to the future value.

To determine the present value of an amount to be paid or received in the future, you simply reverse the future value equation, dividing by the interest factor instead of multiplying by it. The present value of $1 to be received in one year is

$$PV = \frac{\$1}{(1 + r),}$$

where r is the rate of interest. Thus, if the discount rate is 7 percent, the present value of $1 to be received in one year is

$$PV = \frac{\$1}{(1 + .07)}$$

$$= \frac{\$1}{1.07}$$

$$= \$0.93 \text{ (approximately)}$$

Ninety-three cents now is equivalent to $1.00 in one year. If you had 93 cents now and invested it at 7 percent, it would equal $1.00 in one year.

The present value of $1 to be received in two years is

$$PV = \frac{\$1}{(1 + r) \times (1 + r).}$$

The present value of $1 to be received in three years is

$$PV = \frac{\$1}{(1 + r) \times (1 + r) \times (1 + r).}$$

To generalize, the present value of any amount $A to be received in n years is

$$PV = \frac{A}{(1 + r)^n.}$$

For example, if the discount rate is 6 percent, the present value of $750 to be received in 5 years is

$$PV = \frac{\$750}{(1 + .06)^5}$$

$$= \frac{\$750}{(1.06)(1.06)(1.06)(1.06)(1.06)}$$

$$= \$560.44$$

In other words, if your discount rate is 6 percent and we offered to give you $560.44 today or $750 in five years, you wouldn't care because the amounts are equivalent.

This formula can be used to calculate not only the present value of a single amount to be paid or received at one time in the future, but also to calculate the present value of a number of payments to be made at different times. Assume, for example, that an investment would pay you $100 at the end of the first year, $250 at the end of the second year, $50 at the end of the third year, and $400 at the end of the fourth and final year. The present value of this investment is simply the sum of the present values of each payment. If your discount rate is 5 percent, the present value of the first $100 payment, using the formula, is PV = 100/(1.05) = $95.24. The present value of the $250 payment at the end of year two is PV = $250/(1.05)^2 = $226.76 The present value of the $50 payment at the end of year three is PV = 50/(1.05)^3 = $43.19. The present value of the $400 payment at the end of year four is PV = 400/(1.05)^4 = $329.08. The present value of the entire investment is simply the sum of all these individual present values:

$$PV = \frac{100}{(1.05)} + \frac{250}{(1.05)^2} + \frac{50}{(1.05)^3} + \frac{400}{(1.05)^4}$$

$$= \$95.24 + \$226.76 + \$43.19 + \$329.08$$

$$= \$694.27$$

Dealing With Periods Shorter Than a Year

All of the examples so far have involved annual interest rates and periods of exactly one, two, or some number of years. Present values and future values can also be computed for periods of less than one year. The formulas are basically the same:

$$FV = A \times (1 + r)^n$$

$$PV = \frac{A}{(1 + r)^n}$$

where A is the amount to be paid or received, n is the number of periods, and r is the interest or discount rate for each period. However, the period we're now interested in is something other than one year. The "n" in the formula is now the number of days or the number of months or whatever period we want to use and "r" is the interest rate for that period (per day or per month or whatever).

If the *monthly* rate of interest is 1%, the present value of $500 to be received in six months is:

$$PV = \frac{\$500}{(1.01)^6}$$

$$= \$471.02$$

If the *quarterly* rate of interest is 2%, the future value in six months (two quarters) of $10 today is:

$$FV = \$10 \text{ x } (1.02)^2$$

$$= \$10.40$$

The trickiest parts of calculating present values and future values is knowing what period to use and determining the appropriate periodic interest rate. To use the formulas accurately, you need to know how often interest is **compounded**—that is, how often it is credited to the account. Because of compound interest (interest on interest), interest compounded monthly is not the same as interest compounded annually, even though the rates are the same.

Assume that you put $100 each in two different bank accounts. Both accounts pay 12 percent annual interest, but interest is compounded monthly in one account and annually in the other. At the end of one year, the amounts in the two accounts will no longer be the same—the future values will differ.

In the account where interest is compounded annually, nothing will happen until the end of the year. At that point, the bank will calculate your interest (multiplying your $100 by the annual interest rate), and will add the interest to your account. The value of that account after one year will be:

$$FV = \$100 \text{ x } (1 + .12)$$

$$= \$112.00$$

In the account where interest is compounded monthly, the bank will add interest to your account at the end of each month. The monthly interest rate is simply one-twelfth of the annual rate. Thus, at the end of the first month, the amount in your account will be:

$$FV = \$100 \text{ x } (1 + .01)$$

$$= \$101.00$$

At the end of the second month, the bank will again add interest to your account, multiplying the amount in the account by the monthly interest rate. But notice that they're now paying you interest not just on your original $100, but also on the first month's $1.00 interest. You're getting compound interest. At the end of the second month, the amount in your account will be:

$$FV = \$101 \text{ x } (1 + .01)$$

$$= \$102.01$$

We can use the future value formula to calculate how much will be in your account at the end of the year. The number of periods is 12, and the periodic interest rate is 1 percent. The value of the account after one year is:

$$FV = A \times (1 + r)^n$$
$$= \$100 \times (1 + .01)^{12}$$
$$= \$112.68$$

The extra 68 cents (compared to the other account) results from the difference between monthly and annual compounding of interest.

Sixty-eight cents isn't much but, when the amount involved is greater or the number of periods is great, it can make a significant difference. Often, the examples you'll see in law school will assume annual compounding. If not, use the compounding period they specify. If the problem says 12% annual interest, compounded quarterly, use the number of quarters (three-month periods) as "n" and the quarterly interest rate (12 ÷ 4) as "r".

An Application: Lost Wages

The concept of present value is often used to calculate damages, such as the value of lost wages. For example, assume that a defendant is liable to Smith for injuries that left Smith unable to work for the rest of his life. At the time of his injury, Smith was 40 years old; he would have retired at age 65. If Smith was earning $25,000 a year when he was injured and would have continued to earn $25,000 a year for the rest of his life, how much would the defendant have to pay to compensate Smith for his lost wages?[6]

Smith's total wages for the 25 years of work he had remaining would have been $625,000 ($25,000 a year times 25 years). But, due to the time value of money, awarding Smith a lump sum of $625,000 now would drastically overcompensate him. Each $25,000 payment Smith would have received in future years is worth less than $25,000 now. Consider the $25,000 that Smith would have received a year from now. If Smith receives $25,000 now, he could invest it and have more than $25,000 in a year (when he would have received the wages). For example, if Smith could earn 5 percent on an investment, the $25,000 we give him now would become $26,250 ($25,000 x 1.05) in one year.[7] This exceeds what Smith would have had that year if he were working. The

---

[6] To simplify the calculation, we assume a constant wage and no inflation. You could calculate the present value of Smith's lost wages without these assumptions, but you'd have to factor in the expected value and timing of any raises and discount for inflation.

[7] To keep things simple, this calculation assumes that Smith is paid his entire salary once at the end of the year. If Smith's wages are paid on a monthly or weekly basis, we'd have to use a month or a week as our period and use a monthly or weekly discount rate.

$25,000 to Smith for the lost wages two years from now would become $27,562.50 ($25,000 x 1.05 x 1.05) by the time he would have received those wages. Paying Smith $25,000 now for each year of future wages lost overcompensates him.

To accurately measure the present cost to Smith of losing his future wages, we need to discount those wages to a present value. The damages for the wages he would have received next year are not $25,000, but the present value of that $25,000, approximately $23,809 ($25,000 ÷ 1.05). If Smith invests this amount at 5%, he will have exactly $25,000 by the time he would have received the money if he were still working. The damages for the second year's lost wages are the present value of $25,000 to be received in two years, $22,675.74 ($25,000 ÷ 1.05²). If Smith invests this amount, he will have exactly $25,000 by the time he would have earned the second year's wages. If we calculate the present value of each year's wages, we can determine the amount the defendant must pay Smith now to compensate Smith for all of his lost future wages. That amount, assuming a five percent discount rate, is $352,348.61, not $625,000. Notice the big difference a present value calculation can make when payments many years in the future are involved.

The Limits of Present Value and the Value of Sensitivity Analysis

Present value calculations are useful, but they are only as good as the numbers used to calculate them. If you put garbage into the formulas, you get garbage out. No matter how flawless the methodology, the result is meaningless. Used carefully and cautiously, present value calculations are a powerful tool. However, relying on such calculations without careful analysis is just as dangerous as not understanding them at all. As with accounting statements, do not assume that a claim is accurate just because it's dressed up in numbers and mathematics is involved.

Present value calculations depend on the accuracy of (1) the payment amounts, and (2) the discount rate. If the amounts to be paid or received are wrong, the present value will be wrong. Thus, in the preceding example, if Smith's salary for the next 25 years was $30,000 instead of $25,000, the present value we calculated using the $25,000 figure would be meaningless. The present value of his actual wages would be $422,818.34, $70,000 more than our original calculation.

The discount rate used can also have a tremendous effect on present value. The higher the discount rate, the lower the present value. The lower the discount rate, the higher the present value. If, in the previous example, the $25,000 wage figure was correct but the discount rate should have been 7 percent instead of 5 percent, the present value of Smith's wages would be only $291,339.58, a $61,000 difference. The longer the period of time involved, the greater the effect of an improper discount rate.

Fortunately, there is a way to determine how sensitive present values are to the numbers used to calculate them. This process is known as **sensitivity analysis**. To do a sensitivity analysis, you simply input plausible alternative numbers and see how drastically those alternative numbers affect the result. The exact amount of a future payment may be uncertain, but you may be able to calculate a range within which you are sure the amount of the payment will fall. What happens if you use other figures in that range? Similarly, you may not be confident that the discount rate you chose is exactly correct, but you're sure the discount rate falls within a certain range. What happens if you use other rates in that range?

To see how sensitivity analysis works, consider Smith's lost wages again. You believe that Smith's annual salary will be $25,000, but you're uncertain. It could range from $20,000 to $30,000. And your best estimate of the appropriate discount rate is 5%, but it could be anything from 4% to 8%. As we previously saw, given your best estimates ($25,000 and 5%), the present value of Smith's lost wages is approximately $352,349. The following table presents a sensitivity analysis of this calculation.

SENSITIVITY ANALYSIS
PRESENT VALUE OF SMITH'S LOST WAGES

Annual Salary

Discount Rate	$20,000	$25,000	$30,000
4%	$312,442	$390,552	$468,662
5%	$281,879	**$352,349**	$422,818
6%	$255,667	$319,584	$383,501
7%	$233,072	$291,340	$349,608
8%	$213,496	$266,869	$320,243

The table shows what the present value of Smith's lost wages is with various combinations of salary and discount rates. This sensitivity analysis shows how wrong we could be if the actual numbers differ from our best estimates. As you can see, the possible present values vary tremendously—from a high of $468,662 to a low of only $213,496. Given the range of uncertainty, we should be very cautious in using the chosen present value.

19

EXPECTED VALUE

Another useful valuation concept is the concept of **expected value**. Expected value is used to value uncertain outcomes. It is, in essence, an average of the possible outcomes, weighted by the probability that each outcome will occur.

To understand expected value, assume that we offer to bet with you on the roll of a die. We'll roll it once: if a 1 or 2 comes up, we'll pay you $15; if any other number comes up, you have to pay us $9. Should you take this bet?

The outcome when we roll the die is uncertain, but, if the die is fair,[1] each of the six numbers is equally likely. There's a 1/6 chance that a 1 will come up, a 1/6 chance that a 2 will come up, and so on. You win if either a 1 or a 2 comes up, so there's a two out of six, or 1/3, chance that you will win $15. We win if any of the other four numbers comes up, so there's a four out of six, or 2/3, chance that you will have to pay us $9. If we rolled the die again and again, you'd receive $15 approximately 1/3 of the time and you'd pay us $9 approximately 2/3 of the time.

Expected value measures the average outcome of uncertain events such as rolling the die. You calculate expected value by multiplying each possible outcome times the probability that the outcome will occur. Since one of the outcomes *must* occur, all of the probabilities must add up to 1. In the bet example, the two possible outcomes are a $15 win, with a probability of 1/3, and a $9 loss, with a probability of 2/3. The expected value to you of the bet is:

$$EV = (\$15 \times 1/3) + (-\$9 \times 2/3)$$

$$= \$5 + -\$6$$

$$= -\$1$$

On average, you lose $1 on each roll of the die. If we rolled the die an extremely large number of times, you'd win $15 about 1/3 of the time

---

[1] This is probably not a safe assumption if one of the authors furnishes the die. Don't forget that you're betting with a lawyer and an accountant.

and you'd pay $9 about 2/3 of the time, but you'd have an average loss of $1 on each roll. This is not a good bet for you unless you're planning to cheat.

Notice that you never lose exactly $1 on any roll. The only two possibilities are winning $15 or losing $9. The -$1 expected value is only an average, and the average doesn't have to be one of the possibilities (which is why the average family can have 1.9 children even though there are few headless children running around[2]).

Understanding expected value is clearly helpful when you're betting with unsavory law and accounting professors, but what relevance does it have to your legal studies? Consider an example. You represent the plaintiff in a tort case. The defendant's lawyer has offered you $110,000 cash to settle; you're convinced this is her best offer. Should you accept it or try the case? You estimate that the probability of a verdict in favor of the defendant is about 25 percent. There's a 50 percent chance that the plaintiff will win and receive damages of $120,000 and a 25 percent chance that the plaintiff will win and receive damages of $320,000. Assume that it will cost you $20,000 in costs and attorneys' fees to try the case and that, win or lose, each party must pay his own attorneys' fees and costs. The net gain or loss to the plaintiff is the amount of damages received less the costs and attorneys' fees he has to pay. Thus, there's a 25 percent chance that the plaintiff will lose $20,000 ($0 - $20,000), a 50 percent chance that the plaintiff will win $100,000 ($120,000 - $20,000), and a 25 percent chance that the plaintiff will win $300,000 ($320,000 - $20,000). The expected value to the plaintiff of going to trial is:

$$EV = (.25 \times -20,000) + (.50 \times 100,000) + (.25 \times 300,000)$$

$$= -5000 + 50,000 + 75,000$$

$$= \$120,000$$

The expected value of going to trial, $120,000, is greater than the settlement offer, $110,000.

Of course, we've omitted two important elements of valuation that you would want to consider in deciding whether to settle. First, the timing of the payments differs. The settlement will be paid now; the damages won't be paid until sometime in the future, after the conclusion of the trial. To compare the two, you'd want to discount the damages to their present value. Later in this chapter, we'll discuss how to combine present value and expected value in a single calculation. The second consideration is that the settlement amount is fixed and guaranteed.

---

[2] Brainless perhaps, but not headless.

You know for sure what you're getting if you take the settlement. Going to trial is riskier: the plaintiff might win as much as $300,000 or he might lose $20,000. As we'll discuss later, the plaintiff might want to consider this risk in deciding whether to settle.

Expected value analysis is also commonly used in business and government. A government agency might calculate the expected value of adopting a new regulation when it is uncertain what the exact effect of the regulation will be. A business might calculate the expected value of introducing a new product when it is uncertain exactly how profitable the product will be. An investor might calculate the expected value of an investment when the return on the investment is uncertain.

For example, assume that an oil company is deciding whether to drill for oil on property it owns. Drilling will cost $100,000. The company's geologist is not sure if there's oil under the land or, if so, how much oil is there. However, based on her review of the geological data,[3] she can provide some estimates. She thinks there's a 25% chance that the property contains no oil at all, in which case the company incurs the $100,000 cost of drilling and gets no income (a $100,000 loss). There's a 25% chance that the property contains enough oil to produce revenue of $40,000 (a $60,000 loss, after subtracting the cost of drilling). There's a 30% chance that the property contains enough oil to produce revenue of $120,000 (a net profit of $20,000). There's a 20% chance that the property contains enough oil to produce revenue of $300,000 (a net profit of $200,000). To simplify matters, assume that drilling, removing the oil, and selling it all occur instantaneously, so we don't have to worry about calculating present values.[4] The expected value of drilling is

$$EV = (.25 \text{ x } -\$100,000) + (.25 \text{ x } -\$60,000) + (.30 \text{ x } \$20,000)$$
$$+ (.20 \text{ x } \$200,000)$$
$$= \$6,000.$$

If the geologist's estimates are reliable, drilling should be profitable on average.

The Limits of Expected Value and the Use of Sensitivity Analysis

Expected values, like present values, are only as reliable as the numbers used to calculate them. Expected value calculations depend on the accuracy of (1) the possible outcomes and their values and (2) the probabilities assigned to each outcome. If a possible outcome is overlooked or the gain or loss associated with an outcome is misestimated,

---

[3] We use the term "geological data" to disguise the fact that neither of us has the slightest idea what geologists look at.

[4] Or assume that the numbers given are already present values.

the resulting expected value will be unreliable. If the probabilities assigned to each possible outcome are wrong, the resulting expected value will also be wrong. This is an important limitation because it's often difficult to estimate the probabilities of the outcomes. Estimating probabilities is easy when you're rolling dice; it's not as easy when you're drilling for oil or bringing a lawsuit.

Sensitivity analysis can be used to determine how sensitive expected values are to the numbers used to calculate them. A sensitivity analysis of an expected value calculation is done in much the same way as a sensitivity analysis of a present value calculation. You try plausible alternative numbers and see how drastically the alternative numbers affect the result.

To understand how sensitivity analysis works for expected values, reconsider the oil drilling example we looked at earlier. The company's geologist estimates the probabilities of finding oil on the company's property and the associated profit to the company (after subtracting drilling costs) as follows:

No Oil	25%	-$100,000
Some Oil	25%	-$60,000
More Oil	30%	$20,000
Bonanza[5]	20%	$200,000

We calculated earlier that, given these probabilities and outcomes, the expected value of drilling is $6000.

These are the geologist's best estimates of probabilities and outcomes, but she's not absolutely certain of these estimates; she could be wrong. She has calculated three sets of probabilities: her best estimates, a rosy scenario, and a pessimistic scenario, as follows:

	Rosy	Best Estimate	Pessimistic
No Oil	20%	25%	30%
Some Oil	20%	25%	30%
More Oil	35%	30%	25%
Bonanza	25%	20%	15%

The geologist also believes that the profit to the company could vary from her best estimates. Drilling costs might be slightly more or less than her estimates and the price of oil might vary slightly. She has also

---

[5] Given the oil example, a more appropriate label might be "The Beverly Hillbillies." (If you understand this, you need to spend more time studying and less time watching cable T.V.)

calculated rosy and pessimistic scenarios of the returns to the company, as follows:

	Rosy	Best Estimate	Pessimistic
No Oil	-$80,000	-$100,000	-$120,000
Some Oil	-$40,000	-$60,000	-$80,000
More Oil	$40,000	$20,000	$0
Bonanza	$220,000	$200,000	$180,000

We can use the geologist's alternative figures to do a sensitivity analysis. If we combine each of the three sets of probabilities with each of the three sets of monetary outcomes, we can produce nine different expected values. The expected value of each combination appears in the following table:[6]

SENSITIVITY ANALYSIS
EXPECTED VALUE OF OIL DRILLING

Probabilities

Outcomes	Rosy	Best Estimate	Pessimistic
Rosy	$45,000	$26,000	$7,000
Best Estimate	$25,000	**$6,000**	-$13,000
Pessimistic	$5,000	-$14,000	-$33,000

As you can see, although most of the combinations result in gains, the alternative expected values range from a net gain of $45,000 to a net loss of $33,000.

Risk

One problem with using expected values is that they don't take into account **risk**—the variability of the possible outcomes. Two identical expected values can mask very different sets of outcomes.

Pretend that you're a top executive of the Disgusting Toy Company, a toy manufacturer. You have to choose between two proposed toy guns your engineers have designed: the Safety Shooter and the Destructo Destroyer.[7] Each toy costs the same amount to make and the expected value of the profits is the same for both, $10 million. You cannot choose

---

[6] If you want some practice calculating expected values, try to verify one or more of the numbers in the table.

[7] We realize that some parents object to toy guns, but both authors played with toy guns when they were young, and look how they turned out. . . . On second thought, maybe those who object to toy guns have a good point.

one over the other on the basis of expected values because their expected values are the same.

To understand why risk matters, let's look at the probabilities and possible outcomes underlying those identical expected values. The Safety Shooter is a fairly traditional toy. It won't excite the kids too much, but it's a safe, conservative bet. There's a 50 percent chance that it will produce profits of $11 million and a 50 percent chance that it will produce profits of $9 million. Its expected value is:

$$EV = (\$11 \text{ million} \times .5) + (\$9 \text{ million} \times .5)$$
$$= \$5.5 \text{ million} + \$4.5 \text{ million}$$
$$= \$10 \text{ million}$$

The Destructo Destroyer is a much more exciting toy. The kids will love it. Unfortunately, it has a slight problem. The engineers think there's about a 10 percent chance that, after two years' use, the Destructo Destroyers will all blow up, causing great damage (and resulting in great liability for the company). If the Destructo Destroyer works (a 90 percent probability), the profits will be tremendous, approximately $100 million. If it doesn't work and the company has to pay for the injuries (a 10 percent probability), the loss to the company will be approximately $800 million. The Destructo Destroyer's expected value is:

$$EV = (\$100 \text{ million} \times .9) + (-\$800 \text{ million} \times .1)$$
$$= \$90 \text{ million} + -\$80 \text{ million}$$
$$= \$10 \text{ million}$$

The expected values are the same, but the Destructo Destroyer is much riskier; the possible outcomes associated with it are much more variable.

In calculating expected value, $10 million is $10 million. The variability of the possible outcomes—the problem of risk—is not considered. But, in most situations, people don't like risk, everything else being equal. Most people would prefer the Safety Shooter, even though the expected values are the same, because they don't want to risk injuring small children.[8] When you're working with expected values, you should also consider the risk associated with each choice. Risk, like expected value, can be measured, but measurements of risk go beyond the basics to be covered in this book.

Combining Present Value and Expected Value

Present value and expected value calculations are not mutually exclusive. The two can be combined to value uncertain future outcomes.

---

[8] Even we wouldn't have the gall to say "except when those small children are really annoying."

Assume that you're trying to value a possible investment. You have to invest $100 today and you'll receive some amount back in exactly one year. The amount you'll get back is uncertain. You think there's a 50% chance that you'll only get your original $100 back. There's a 25% chance that you'll do better and receive $250 back, and a 25% chance that you'll get nothing at all, not even the $100 you originally invested.

To value this investment, you first need to translate the possible future receipts into present values. Assume that your discount rate is 10 percent. The present value of the $100 outcome is

$$PV = \frac{100}{(1 + .10)}$$

$$= \$90.91.$$

The present value of the $250 outcome is

$$PV = \frac{250}{(1 + .10)}$$

$$= \$227.27.$$

The present value of the $0 outcome is

$$PV = \frac{0}{(1 + .10)}$$

$$= \$0.[9]$$

Now that we have converted each possible outcome into a present value, we can calculate an expected value of those present values, or **expected present value**. We do this in the same way we calculate any other expected value, by multiplying each outcome by its probability and adding the products. The expected present value of the investment is

$$EPV = (.5 \times \$90.91) + (.25 \times \$227.27) + (.25 \times 0)$$

$$= \$102.28.$$

Since you invest only $100 and get back an average of $102.28, this is a profitable investment (ignoring the risk of the investment).

Notice that we calculated present values first, then calculated an expected value of those present values. If all of the possible outcomes occur at the same time, you can do the calculation in the opposite order—first doing the expected value calculation, then converting that result into a present value. However, when the different outcomes occur

---

[9] The present value of any zero outcome is always zero.

at different times, this won't work, so we suggest you always do the present value part of the calculations first.

INDEX